Foreword & Disclaimer

It is being said that we are the sum of our experiences. I believe that this is incomplete. The more valid statement is:
We are the sum of our experiences and the experiences of those we learn from. In that state of mind, this book is written.

While the lessons contain my personal experiences of 14+ years of digital success and failures at UCB Pharma, Schwarz Pharma, Johnson & Johnson, Janssen Pharmaceuticals as well as mentoring & engaging with start-ups in different industries, more importantly, it contains the teachings that were shared with me by my mentors, colleagues, and my family. This book in its entirety contains my own opinions and at no point reflects the views of my current or previous employers.

The entire book was written on my mobile devices via werdsmith.com, grammar checked by grammarly.com, the front page designed in kindle create, and published via kindle direct self-publishing.

While this book is written with a linear story in mind, **the best way to read this book is to jump back and forth to the sections that create value for you personally** and skip those that are not.

Welcome to the Casino of Digital

Las Vegas. The place where dreams are made; or destroyed. The Vegas strip. Hotels. Lights festivals everywhere. From the show in front of the Bellagio where water fountains engulfed in light dance to the rhythm of "time to say goodbye", to the lights of casinos promising eternal riches & fame. It is a place for blender and spender. A city that has born probably more losers than winners over decades, yet its attraction to the masses is still enormous.

You are part of this city. Attracted by its ideas and hopes for the great returns and a better life. In one of the big casinos, you are finding yourself.

You are at the poker table surrounded by people you barely know. A private room surrounded by Vegas typical casino lights, promising suspense.
Seven players, each holding two cards. Some visibly stressed, feeling overwhelmed. Some showing off, acting like kings as the know-it-all. Some not even picking up the cards just believing they do not need the cards to win. The dealer is revealing the cards on the table. You have your drink in your left and your cards in your right.

You hold a blockchain card and an artificial intelligence card in your hand. On the table is a cloud card, a digital transformation card, and a wearables card.

Do you fold? Do you raise, how much? Do you bluff? Will you win?

It is hard today to know if you are holding the right cards. Do you even know the rules which hand is better in today's world? Is there only one blockchain card? Is artificial intelligence maybe just a buzz word and worth nothing? Or is it the joker that you need?

You sit, you sweat, you wait. Some players announce to the room they have the best cards in the world, some players stare at the table, some people get out of the game saying they don't need these "modern cards", some folding because "technologies are evil". Some raise the stakes because a consultant told them that one of their cards with "technology X is the best in the world".

In the end, a Silicon Valley or Dragon Valley player enters the game and shows a royal flush; you lost and do not even know why.

This feeling and the behavior of the different players is what we see in the day to day business management around digital. From fears of technology to digital bullshit bingo to consulting overkill promoting best practices that are outdated when they reach you, to the blenders who talk a lot and say nothing, the ignorant and to the disrupters.

Technology knowledge in the past belonged to the experts, to the geeks, the IT departments to the few. But now such an approach cannot be afforded anymore today. You do not need to know how a car works to drive it. If you do not know the difference between a car, a boat, and a plane you will have a tough time deciding how much you should spend on each or use each.

I grew up a time where "digital" was uncool. Seriously. Telling someone at a date you build facial recognition software as a child, ended each date rather quickly. Now it gets you invited to yacht parties and conferences. Times have changed. We need to adapt. And the first step to adapting is understanding.

Over the next chapters, I will take you on a small journey of misunderstandings, knowledge, risks, and opportunities when it comes to the digital gamble.

What do you do when **the deck is stacked,** and **the odds** are against you?

The odds of playing the game

Possibilities, Success, Failures

A few years ago, a couple of friends invited me to a small family party at their hotel suite. They had an amazing suite, flowers pots larger than my tv at that time, an infinite pool partially inside and partially outside a larger terrace, and an elevator that went directly into their room. It was partially surreal. The members of the party were a great mix of backgrounds, age groups, and professions. From engineers to bankers to kindergarten teachers to civil servants. A couple of them brought their kids ranging from 5 to 15 years old. While standing in line at the perfectly prepared buffet, I saw one child that build Lego cars. Bypassing him I asked what he is building. He said cars. I asked him if he likes building new things. Seeing the bewilderment in the eyes of the 10-year-old, I tried to explain: I told him that I always enjoyed as a child using Lego to create new worlds, new ideas, and new objects.

He said:

"But everything exists already, I only build what the instructions say". In other words, everything that can be created has been created.

I think I left the child at this moment cause the situation created such a cognitive dissonance for me. The belief of people that nothing else can be invented broke my mind.

So, I went out in search if I can prove that the opposite is true. I went into the area that is most natural to me. The digital realm.

Could I find a way to prove to myself that the invention possibilities are infinite and that nothing is impossible?

I went back to the basics in all my thinking and started with how are computer engineered. If you take everything away it is basically all 0s and 1s. Each 0 presents a switch being off and each 1 represents a switch being on.

In other words, imagine a light switch in your room, that you can turn off (0) and on (1). Now imagine that by switching on and off your light switch in a certain order and a certain rhythm you can create a calculator. By continuing with a different rhythm and different timing and sequence repetition you can create the websites, artificial intelligence, online payment systems, blockchains, you can create a website where Micky Mouse is singing a blues in the voice of Britney Spears while playing basketball with Michael Jordan. All that by just turning on and off your light switch. By just having 0 and 1. Nothing else is needed. Once you agree with your neighbor on a common language what a certain light switch sequence means and they observe the light from your window that they see at night and do the same, light on and light off, you will realize that you just created the internet. You established a few protocols and started exchanging information over a larger and larger network. First text with your 0 & 1, then datasets that can be translated into voice and later into a video. All you need is a light switch. Our complete economy & society is today built on an army of light switches that turn on and off at lightning-fast speed. There is no magic and that is the magic.

I was realizing that an infinite number of 0101 combinations exist and that with an infinite number of 0 and 1 you can create everything that can be imagined and everything that no one has ever imagined. This reemphasized one of the key facts when it comes to digital.

Impossible is impossible. There is nothing a computer cannot do; it just means that sometimes we have not yet found the right sequence of 00111001 that can create it.

It gave me the confidence that there is no problem too hard and no idea too complicated that it cannot be solved. We can create complete worlds online, interact everywhere, we have currencies that have no physical counterpart, thus existing only in the digital world, we have the world's knowledge available when and where we need it and we might even have the key for eternal life.

We have access to technology that creates infinite possibilities. We are only limited by our mind, not the technology. Everything we have today in the digital world from blockchain to AI could have existed 20 years ago. It might have run slower but so did everything at that time. The only limitation of the number of creations and the solutions to problems is our imagination.

Impossible is impossible. This is a key I kept in mind in everything I do.

Too often I have heard that
- Technology cannot do this
- Artificial intelligence is stupid it could not solve this problem
- Only humans can do this task
- It is impossible to create something like this.

We also remember similar statements in other contexts
- Taxis: Uber will not work
- Hotels: Airbnb will not work
- Retail: Amazon will not work
- Banks: Bitcoin will not work

Now every time I hear this I smile and think to myself that we just have not had the right imagination & mind to solve it. Then I imagine that the same persons that complained about technology projects saying something is impossible, that when they come home and turn on and off the light in their bedroom they actually have the key infinite possibilities at their fingertips. Literally.

'Everything we hear is an opinion, not a fact. Everything we see is a perspective, not the truth.' Marcus Aurelius

Success & Failure

I read in the news that 70% of all digital transformations fail. If we look at the numbers published in the past years by CNBC this has reached 1.3 trillion in investment leading to 800 billion dollars that are being spent without creating value. Some surveys say it is 85%, some say it is 60%. And out of the successful digital transformation programs, only 16% saw a concrete performance improvement. In any case, it seems that digital transformation seems hard work with often little reward.

7 successful & unsuccessful digital transformations in companies

What do Hasbro, Nike, Home Depot, Honeywell, BestBuy, and Disney have in common? They had successful digital transformations.

Hasbro adjusted their business model to attract customers via digital storytelling, video content, social media presence, combined with nostalgic brands. They learned how to use data better than their competition to anticipate the needs of customers. They also harnessed the power of digital storytelling through social media and video content.
Since their digital transformation, the company stock climbed from 36$ to 109$. They were able to increase sales by over 1 billion by e.g. increasing their investments in digital ads by 1100%.

Nike was a few years back in a less than optimal position. Despite having a strong customer base and specifically brands like their Air Jordan were still selling well it felt like the brand was slipping with limited growth in both share price and revenue. In 2010, Nike created a digital division called Nike Digital Sport. They focused on a complete digital transformation on mindset, supply chain, branding, online presence adjusting their business model towards more direct to consumer online sales, new revenue streams through subscription models, concept stores, and mobile app experiences like create your own shoe personalization online. Within the first two years of the transformation, their share price jumped 44%. It is additionally a nice example of resilience as well as learning as a few years prior invested 400m in a new ERP system resulting in a write off of 100m with a stock price drop of 20% - requiring another 400m dollar to get the project back on track.

Honeywell's share price jumped from 95$ to 174$ using new internal digitization and expanding its offering to include more technology solutions. While also completely reinventing their industrial process control.

A few years back Home Depot hired 1000 digital professionals with a focused group on customer experience. They rejuvenated their IT department, especially reusing customer data, making sure inventory is optimal and they are identifying early trends faster than the competition. Their stock value was growing from 135$ to 215$ and their revenue grew by more than 17 billion dollars.

BestBuy is an electronic retailer focused on the US market. A few years back they were destined to become the next "Blockbuster level disaster". The majority of experts believed that there was simply no space for them with amazon, apple, and others dominating the tech markets. Yet with a major shift of new business model changes and unique pricing & value focus, they were able not only to survive but to strife.
They introduced a price matching program and switched its focus to advising customers instead of previously just selling to them. BestBuy offers in-home consultations on how customers can best use their devices, and the Geek Squad will now fix anything in a customer's home for a flat annual subscription fee allowing a steady income of revenue.

A few amazing cases of winners of the digital gamble.

	Years duration of digital transformation	Stock Price growth
Hasbro	7	203%
BestBuy	7	198%
Honeywell	3	83%
Nike	2	69%
Target	8	66%
Homedepot	2	59%

They were successful where others failed. As on the other side, many companies failed in their digital transformation. While the hidden names are numerous, few are known. The few that are becoming apparent are either as they caused public lawsuits between different parties or because of a major impact on the share price.

You can find different type of failed transformation projects; some internal single project digitization projects as Haribo, Hershey, Nike, US Navy, Waste management, and major transformations like especially GE, PG, and Ford.

Single digital project failure is usually become apparent due to a major lawsuit or stock price slide.

- For Haribo failure meant that in multiple geographies their gummy bears were not available in 2018, after implementing their SAP system. They spend a massive amount to fix their supply chain as they had no more tracking for inventory, no deliveries and sales dropped 25%
- Washington community college in 2012 was sued by their digital implementation partner PeopleSoft for 13m dollar

- HP invested 160m in a new ERP system resulting in a loss of 600m due to a series of small problems creating a perfect storm
- American National Grid paid 1b dollar in a comparable failure and even the US navy has spent over 1b since 1998 on a single digitalization project with no confirmed improvements since.

But the more interesting cases are the ones that try a holistic transformation and fail at those.

GE in 2011 started a major digital transformation initiative by building a massive IoT platform and changing its business model for industrial products.
In 2015 it took the next step by building a new company decision called "GE Digital". The goal was to turn GE with all data available into a digital key player. The unit had billions in Opex (operational expenses) and a massive number of individuals working on the transformation. Yet they had little directed focus as they tried to do everything at once. The company share price dropped and the CEO was soon kindly asked to leave.

Procter & Gamble in 2012 set out to become "the most digital company on the planet". The industry-leading PG was hoping to take their market dominance to a new level using digital transformation. Unfortunately, a vision alone was not enough if the individual initiatives lagged purpose leading to a downfall and the forced resignation of the CEO. A key lesson was that leadership and strategy as well as tactical focus is key. Going digital for the sake of digital will fail. Transforming for the sake of transforming will fail. You need a purposeful, targeted, and focused transformation strategy.

Ford in 2014 created a new department called "Ford smart mobility" with the focus of building digitally-enabled cars. Yet it was managed largely independently of the rest of the organization. Both physically, as the HQ of the department was far located from the rest of the organization, as well as structurally with no matrix or cultural connection to the rest of the company. With money drained of some parts of the organization to leading to downsides in the Ford core business and not gaining upsides in their new venture. Resulting in a stock price drop and the resignation of the CEO.

7 failure probabilities of investments

After analyzing news, annual reports, lawsuits (amazing level of detail of information), and share price evolution of 50+ companies the 70% failure rate did have some indices going for it. Yet the number seemed still high. After thinking about it, I was realizing that I cannot compare these numbers without looking at different industries, different types of investments, and different types of transformations. Is a digital transformation failure rate of 70% comparably high or low?

If you don't like reading about probabilities best jump to page 30. Don't worry, I will not take it personally.

So, I started my research by looking at what are the failure rates per industry of any start-up after 5 years. The first fact I found was that 90% of start-ups fail within their first 10 years. Yet if we look at the break down after 5 years, we see significant differences between industries. The industry with the lowest failure rate of start-ups was the art & entertainment industry with a 33% failure rate followed by the healthcare industry with 40% of companies failing within 5 years of conception followed by the food industry with 50%. On the other side of the spectrum, you find on the 2nd highest failure rate industry construction with 53% and only topped by IT/Digital Companies with 63%. After reviewing the numbers, it made sense looking at the massive speed in the digital space, the low entry cost, and the high innovation turnover that only 37% of companies in the tech industry are alive after year 5.

These numbers seemed to be supporting the theory of the "70% of digital transformation project fail" quite a bit. Why would not almost the same amount of digital transformation fail vs newly created companies.

Yet I still felt I needed to evaluate also different types of investments and wanted to look at their probability of success. So, I started analyzing the failure rate of:

- Transformations (Cultural transformations, Organization Transformation, Business model transformation)
- Investment options of companies (Saving Account, Website creation, ERP system implementation, General IT Project, Mobile APPS, New Product R&D, Development of Medicine)
- Gambling (Lotto, Blackjack, Roulette, Poker)
- Non-business transformation (Diet, Pregnancy)

To ensure that I can compare the failure rate I wanted to dive into an area where failure and success are just a thin line: Gambling.

Casinos make millions and many countries finance a large amount of their budget due to the tax income of gambling. If you have ever been to Vegas, you know what I mean. The bank always wins. Or so goes the saying. But what do the numbers tell us? Spending the time to analyze what are your chances to succeed while being in Vegas and if the probability of winning in the casino is higher than winning at a digital transformation project?

Let us look at the 4 most popular games when it comes to gambling. Slot machines are excluded in this analysis as I found out that the different games on slots can have varying winning odds. Rather I focused on blackjack, poker, roulette and to add a non-Vegas gamble Lotto, specifically the Euro Jackpot.

The Euro Jackpot is a pan-European lottery in which you need to select 5 numbers out of 50 plus 2 additional numbers out of 10. Thus, you might select 1,5,33,48,49 + 4,5. If the jackpot is filled fully, which we will assume in this argument, you would gain 90.000.000 Euro with an investment of as little as 2 Euro. Your probability of success is 1:95,344,200 or a success rate of 0.000001%.

Roulette might be one of the most iconic games in gambling that you know. The sound of the ball that is spinning in one direction and the underlying wheel spinning in the other direction. "No more bets". The ball stopping on a field between the number of 0 to 37. All even numbers are black and all uneven are red. With the 0 being the only green number. Before you spin the ball, you must choose where to bet. You can bet on red or black so that when the ball falls on a number matching your color you will gain twice what you have invested. You can also play lanes, or you can play areas of e.g. 6 numbers in combination or you can play an individual number. This means that if you for example bet all your money on 27, you will get 36 times all the money you invested.
If you play the strategy of always playing red or black you have a probability of winning of 48.6%. It would be 50/50 if it would not be for the green 0.
If you play a single number, you have a probability of winning of 2.7%.

Blackjack might be known as the game of 21. On a blackjack table, you always compete against the bank, no matter how many players are on the table. Each player gets two cards and can request more cards afterward. The goal is to get as close as possible to 21. With 21 leading to a blackjack. Should the player exceed 21 they fail. Should they stay below 21 they can hold, and their result will be compared to the dealer cards. Whoever has the higher card sum but stays below or equal to 21 wins the hand. This will lead to a doubling of your bet.

The probability of you winning any given hand in a normal deck without seeing your cards is roughly 48%.

The fourth game I was looking at was Poker. Casino Royale. James Bond. Such an iconic game. Often used as lessons for business and mathematics.

Now poker success rate is a bit harder to calculate considering that you are playing other players. While it is easy to calculate the winning chances of each hand after you were dealt with them, doing it before is much harder. Let us look at the World Series of Poker. One of the most prestigious tournaments that there are. A multi-day event will end with one person out of 8777 participants to walk away with 12.000.000 Dollars, a ring, and eternal bragging rights.

For the time being, we will use an easy probability of 1:8777 that you will win the tournament (0,011%)

So, looking at these odds' Digital transformation success is in between blackjack or a black/red color roulette strategy and roulette (single digit strategy) or poker or the lottery.

Considering this I felt that all my time spent studying business was becoming irrelevant. How can it be that having your CEO take all your company assets going to Vegas and putting them on red has a higher chance of success for your company than running your digital transformation?

Yet I was wondering where other business investments fall in this spectrum. After research, if found following statistics

- 90% of employee training programs fail, as only 10% of employees gained and retained the taught skill after one year
- 75% of all ERP projects, rolling out e.g. SAP in your company, fail, as being defined as scope not delivered (over budget or delayed projects count still as success)
- 90% of all websites fail within the first 120 days

- 88% of new drugs developed by pharma companies never make it to the market despite on average needing to spend 1.8 Billion USD per drug
- 70% of mobile apps fail in the first year and only 0.03% of apps will ever make more than 1m in Revenue. To date out of 1m apps, only 300 apps including Fortnite, Netflix, Tinder are falling in this category
- 48% of all IT projects do not meet their primary goals
- 70% of organization transformation fail
- 66% of structural transformation fail
- 70% of cultural transformations fail
- 80% of new product innovations fail

After reading this I had two key insights. One, I now understand why asking your CFO for money is hard. Two, that the idea of sending the CEO to Vegas does not sound so stupid anymore. You could of course also leave the money on your savings account and have a 99% chance that you do not lose it, but it does not evolve.

Does this also apply to our private life? If you ever went on a diet you know what failure looks like. 95% of all people that went on a diet had regained or passed their weight of one year ago.
Between 2006 and 2016 64% of all US mortgages failed which caused the financial crisis.
Even our most natural life-giving process has a failure rate with 20% of all pregnancies fail.

This gave me great optimism. Why? Because I realized that failing truly is part of life and that failure is far from a sign of weakness, but a sign of evolution.
Everyone who talks about failure and thinks failure is not natural or that failure is rare has been blinded by our Instagram and social media world.

Only 1 type of person never fails. Those that do not try. Yet we are so influenced to always show our great side that we lose a view on reality. Many of my friends post the most beautiful messages and picture on Instagram every day! Even when I know they are miserable. We do fail every day and failing is far from the problem.

Looking at the overall failure rates we get a picture like this:

Name	Probability of Success
Saving Account	99%
IT projects (internal applications)	52%
Roulette (choose black or red)	48,6%
Blackjack	48%
Company Transformation	30%
Digital Transformation	30%
Organization Transformation	30%
Mobile Apps	30%
ERP Projects	25%
New products	20%
Websites(advertisement)	13%
Clinical Trials for new drugs	12%
Websites (eCommerce physical product)	10%
Start-Ups	10%
Employee Training 90%	10,00%
Websites (eCommerce digital product)	7%
Diet	5%
Roulette (select individual number)	2,70%
World Series Poker Tournament	0,011399%
Lotto (EuroJackpot)	0,000001%

Let us dive further into this failure rate and how to choose what we want to do.

The probability of success is only a part of discussing failure. The other side is what we can gain if we were to succeed. In other words, what is the ROI if we would succeed. Cause if we just want to minimize our risk, we will just keep the money on the bank's savings account. Here you might get 1.5% in good years.

The easiest example here is the lottery. With 2 Euro of investment, you can gain up to 90.000.000 Euro return which means you have an ROI of 45.000.000 Euro. For new drugs, you will have roughly an ROI of 15x (dropping towards 10x over the next few years) your investment.

The bestselling mobile app game Fortnite creates a revenue of 1.8 billion, while average games that create more than 1 million in revenue have a yearly cost of 250.000 leading to an ROI of 4 on average.

Blackjack winnings have an ROI of 2:1, same as the color strategy of roulette.

The single number strategy of roulette gives you a 36:1 pay-out.

IT projects of internal applications have usually a 175% ROI after 3 years.

The World Series of poker requires a 10k buy-in and pays 12m leading to an ROI of 120000%.

If we combine both ROI and probability, we can calculate how much return an average investment of 1.000.000 brings you given their probability %. In other words, considering the probability of success and the potential return of the 1 million how much money will make you. We will use the below formula:

Probabilistic Return
$$= ROI \times Investment \times Probability$$

Let us look at roulette in this case.
- If you went with the same color strategy you will gain 2x your investment (1.000.000) at a probability of

48.7% leading to 972.972 Euro on average after playing.

*2(ROI) * 1.000.000(Investment) * 48.7(Probability) = 972.972*

- If you went with the single number strategy e.g. you place your money on the number 27. If you play long enough you will gain 36 million at a probability of 2,7% resulting in an average of you guessed it 972.972 Euro.

*36(ROI) * 1.000.000(Investment) * 2.7(Probability) = 972.972*

This means when enough players play roulette no matter which strategy you play on average the Bank gains out per player 27k. For blackjack, it is a loss of 40k per player.

In the Euro Jackpot out of a one million euro gamble, you come out with 471k thus losing roughly 53% of your investment.

For the World Series of Poker is only a 0,01% chance with an ROI of 120.000% this still on average only leads to a 133k pay-out out of your 1m investment.

*120 (ROI) * 1.000.000(Investment) * 0.0114% (Probability) = 133.000*

Therefore, casinos are striving. Therefore, the bank always wins.
From the starting block, you are set up for failure. Even when you are winning from time to time. The longer you play the more likely you lose. Just to ensure that there are not a few lucky winners that leave the casinos after winning a bit, you are being encouraged to continue. You get some free drinks; the air is fresh and the light in the casino is made so that you do

not follow the time. And over time all your winnings become losses.

So how do our chances look like when doing projects in the company.

IT projects have usually an ROI (efficiency-driven) of 175% at a probability of 52% leading to an investment return of 910k.

*1.75 (ROI) * 1.000.000(Investment) * 52% (Probability) = 910k*

Mobile Apps today have a 30% chance to be successful and have an average ROI of 84% meaning that you are losing roughly 75% of your investments.

The probability to create an app that reaches 50m Euro in revenue per year is 0,03% and even with a 20.000% ROI on average you only get 63k back thus lose 94% of your 1 million investment.

*20 (ROI) * 1.000.000(Investment) * 0,03% (Probability) = 60k*

When discussing websites, the ROI depends largely on the type of business model used, splitting into 3 main categories:

- Websites income based on advertisement 13% success rate with an ROI of 162%
- Websites e-commerce physical products 10% success rate with an ROI of 188%
- Websites e-commerce digital products 7% success rate with an ROI of 480%

If we look at all the projects in the research the only two positive investments when looking at the probabilistic return are a savings account (1m become 1.015m) and Drug development which have had a return of converting 1m to

1,8m. The key problem with drug development is the large entry constraints of both legislation and requiring at least 1.8 billion in cash burn before bringing a drug to market. All other investments lead usually to losses of between 4% and 90%. With IT projects resulting in almost the same return as the blackjack table.

What if this is true about digital transformation? What is the ROI of digital transformation? If we follow a view surveys done by consulting companies like the ROI in the next year will be 117% thus converting your investment of 1m into 1.17m in the next year to 1.6m in year three. They interviewed many different CIO & CEOs to derive this.

Should this be true, using the simple formula we have, this means that all our digital transformation strategies are doomed.

If digital transformations have a 70% failure rate, we need to design each digital transformation project to have an ROI of a minimum of 333% to even the odds of having a positive investment return

Name	Probability of Success	ROI	If you invest 1.000.000
Clinical Trials for new drugs	12%	1500%	1.800.000
Saving Account	99%	102%	1.004.850
Roulette (select individual number)	2,70%	3600%	972.972
Roulette (choose black or red)	48,6%	200%	972.972
Blackjack	48%	200%	960.000
IT projects (internal applications)	52%	175%	910.000
Lotto (EuroJackpot)	0,000001%	4500000000%	471.974
ERP Projects	25%	175%	437.500
Company Transformation	30%	117%	351.000
Digital Transformation	30%	117%	351.000
Organisational Transformation	30%	117%	351.000
Websites (ecommerce digital product)	7%	480%	336.000
Mobile Apps	30%	84%	252.400
Websites (advertisement)	13%	162%	210.600
Websites (ecommerce physical product)	10%	188%	187.826
World Series Poker Tournament	0,011399%	120000%	136.783

Does that mean that doing digital transformation is the wrong thing from the perspective of financial management? No. It means the opposite. It means we need to play the odds differently.

Our companies are not casinos. We can change both the odds as well as the pay-out. We cannot change the ROI of the lottery. We cannot change the odds of winning the lottery. We cannot change the odds of blackjack unless you are illegally counting cards. We cannot change the pay-out of roulette.

But we can influence the probability of winning the World Series. By knowing when to play your hand, when to raise, how to read your opponent, and how to bluff you can raise your chance of winning drastically. If you are 8x as good as the average player in the tournament you have a good probability coming home with more than what came with.

Yet contrary to poker where we can change the probability of success, but not the ROI, we can move the two levers of our equation for our digital or business transformation: The ROI (ambition) and the probability of success.

Studies around both start-ups, as well as internal projects, have shown that those that fail once have a 20% higher chance of succeeding the second time and a 30% higher chance of succeeding than at their first attempt. Unfortunately, most fail once and do not try again. Their egos are too badly hurt, and their confidence is shattered largely due to the negative feedback provided by the people around them. One of my mentors once confronted me with the following when asking him "when is the right moment to stop": "When your child falls on their nose when trying to walk, after how many times do you tell him/her to stop trying? You would not do it, no matter how hard other parents or kids are laughing. If the value of achievement is outweighing the probability of failing - there is only one course of action - Repeat, Fail, Learn and Try until you succeed"

"If the value of achievement is outweighing the probability of failing - there is only one course of action - Repeat, Fail, Learn and Try until you succeed"

This leads us to two different strategies when going towards a digital transformation that we see in the industry.

a) You do focus on a **small ROI** but **increase the probability** of success but taking lower risk projects; have experts joining that have required expertise and follow the best practice

b) You **increase the ROI** drastically while controlling your failure chance even if it means you only have 10% or lower chance of success. If you think about a disrupting vision that has an ROI of 100x even a 2% probability of success is worth the investment.

If we follow our math how long will it take you to reach a successful project outcome?

If you run 50 projects you will succeed at least in one of them.

The failure formula

Personally, I always believed in the second option of focusing on maximizing the ROI. Do not focus on minimizing the risk, focus on maximizing the return. If you fail often enough and do not be discouraged but encouraged eventually you will succeed. SpaceX, Tesla, Google, Amazon. Everyone fails, which is why they succeed.

What is SpaceX's most viewed video?

"How to not land an orbit rocket booster" - Celebrated the explosions of their aircraft, slipping radar stations but ending with the 1st successful ever drone rocket landing on a boat barely large enough to hold it. Wonderful visual of failing your way to success in the most spectacular way possible.

If each time that we fail, we learn, and if we just get 10% better than we were before, we would need only 19 projects to succeed at a 100x idea.

Different people learn at different ranges but when analyzing projects especially reruns projects are between 10-30% more successful than previous projects. This is true for companies, projects, and start-ups. Start-up owners that failed once are 16% more probable than others to succeed at their next start-up.

Always fail, always learn, but if you can also learn from other's failures and successes - steal with pride. In the next section, we look to identify which companies succeeded in digital and which once failed as well as seeing what I could learn from them.

Many companies like GE, PG, and Ford failed. Yet which of these were a failure? I firmly believe that none of the companies above are a failure I believe especially in the area of digital transformation that there are companies that succeed, there are companies that give up and there are those that have simply not yet found how to win.

In a later chapter we will look later at what these companies did differently and how leadership, strategy, organization structure impact the success rate of digital transformation to improve the odds at winning. But before this, we need to look at a few more fundamental items that influence our success.

CHANGE, PERSPECTIVE & CHOICE

What makes humans unique on the planet? Two elements that have been developing during thousands of years of evolution: Choice and a free mind.

The combination of change and ability of choice is one of humankind's' biggest paradoxes. In every aspect, it is a double-edged sword. If we use it wisely it can unleash all our potential. Or it can completely block and destroy us.
It is being said that humans are one of the few species on earth that do not live to their fullest potential. The ability of choice is allowing us to choose to fulfill or not to fulfill our potential in each environment.

How high does a tree grow? As high as it can

No tree ever stopped growing if it had enough water, space, and sunlight. So how come that even if our environment allows up to strive that we might decide to go against change & choose the path of status quo.
In our companies and more importantly in our lives we need to take an active choice to step out of the tragedy of missed opportunities. Digital transformation is key in the evolution of any company, yet we often choose not to commit. We always have a choice; one that allows us to choose unimaginable transformations as well as to choose the status quo.

Transformation is defined as a massive change to a person, an organization, an ecosystem, or other entities.
In other words:

$$Transformation = Change^2$$

Unfortunately choosing to transform is a massive effort and maintaining that choice can become a colossal mountain of work. Even if you choose the path it does not mean you will be able to see success immediately. Anyone who ever tried a diet has seen this.

We all have a choice of what to eat when to eat, how much sport we do, and how we live our life. Out of 100 people that want to change, only 33 are actually "choosing" to start the diet, even if they believe their bodies need it.

Choosing to start is a great first step. But what happens usually is that afterward out of the 33 only 10 are continuing with the diet after a few weeks. One of two things happen for most:

a) A large group realizes that change is hard and stop
b) We do not see any immediate change and miss the instant gratification

Especially the second point you have probably seen a million times yourself. I talk about your friend that will go one time into the gym and spend the next day looking in the mirror if the muscles have grown. I talk about your friends that two days stopped eating junk food and are upset that on the scale they have not lost weight. I talk about your boss that is talking about transformation but complains about missing short term results on their bottom line.

Patience is a virtue; Persistence a requirement; and vision is your lifeblood of any change you want to achieve

---

A colleague of mine tried to enrich this misunderstanding about digital transformation with an old tale from the Far East.

The story is taking place in a small village with only a few hundred villagers living there. Most of the villagers grew fruits each season. Planting seeds in autumn and harvesting in spring. Supported by good weather and a good future the village was prospering. But like any village, there is one odd person. One stranger. One crazy one. A farmer who is like many of the others that one day stopped planting their daily fruits but chose a new type of seeds.

Every day he went and watered the seeds. After the first spring still no sign of growth. The village was making fun of him.

You are watering the earth for nothing.

You should have stayed with the plants you know.

You waste your time.

Yet the farmer stayed persistent and just smiled. Every day. This continued for 4 years and everyone thought about the crazy farmer in the village.

In the 5th year. The seeds had developed in 5 weeks 10-meter-high bamboo trees. Bamboos which was able to be turned into houses, boats, materials, bridges, and many more. It took a short time after that that the crazy farmer became the most searched in the village and prospered more than anyone around.

The question is: Did the bamboo grow in 5 weeks 10 meters or 5 years?

Many villagers tried to repeat what the farmer had done but when after 5 weeks they did not see the success they stopped and reverted to their old ways. Persistence, Vision, and Patience. No change will ever come without the three.

(Tactic) TYR - Transformative Yet Recognisable

The second biggest paradox in the world is that people love to change as much as they hate it. You need change but if it comes, you are upset by it.

If we do not change, we will be changed or disrupted by someone else. In private as well as in business.

Is it not confusing how at a time where we preach change, innovation, and disruption, we are so uncomfortable in a situation where change happens to us? Changing the location or changing jobs is hard. No one is celebrating when they lost their job.

You constantly have a feeling of loss and uncomfortably that sits deep in your gut. You have probably seen your own managers preach how change is needed but are personally clinging to what they are used too.

The most successful companies are the most innovative.

So how come that some innovations are more successful than others how could the iPhone, cloud systems, AI systems, or even new concepts like design thinking gain such momentum. Are they more transformative than others? Or maybe they are less?

Like in many parts of life timing is everything.

Why did Apple invest the iPod before the iPad? Why did AI systems only now come into play even if the technology behind is quite old? Why after the horse, did we not jump directly to self-driving cars? Before apple developed its health applications, google already had a „google health kit" but it got decommissioned years before Apple even started and had such a major success in that area.

Innovation happens at the verge between things you know, or things you recognize and things you do not know.

Imagine a line. Half the line are things you know /you(or your customer) have seen and heard about. And half are things you do not know.

Next, you can place each product or service on this line.

Any product that at the time of launch is purely in the transformative part of the line is something that is massively new (Project 1). The prediction is that it will fail, and it will not reach your critical mass of customers as too much education is needed.

Any product that is in the recognizable part of the line is something that your customers know (Project 2). The prediction is that it will fail, and you just reinvented the wheel.

The solution your product needs is that it will need to reach partly in what your customer knows and partly in what is new (Project 3). Any product you develop needs to have at least some anchor in the "what is recognizable" part. This anchor can be build based on your own brand. The iPad anchored in the iPhone and the iPhone anchored in the iPod.

The iPod was anchored in the MP3 player and the disk man as well as the design focus of Apple towards the artists and creatives of the world.

The higher the % of transformative coverage the higher the gain and the lower the probability of success.

This concept is called TYR, transformative yet recognizable. For all your internal and external products, you will try to maximize the transformative coverage, but you must find what your anchor is. Which existing customer knowledge or belief are you anchoring your product/service at? Find that answer and even the craziest concepts will be a major success.

This is not a concept that applies to business only but to life itself.
If you lose your job you lose your anchor. If you change locations, you cannot find an anchor in the new environment then it probably will be hard for you to adopt. Thus, it is easier to move to a country that speaks your language or has the same religion and culture than some truly different culture.

The last key element is in this model is time. The evaluation of a product on recognisability and transformation is changing over time (in general moving towards the right). iPod in 2010 had great transformational value with some recognizable features. The same in 2020 would be a complete disaster. Google was too early in its health kit by not having a customer anchor.

One of my teachers kept telling me in university that the „first to market is always getting most of the market share". Meanwhile, I believe that to be successful you need to be the first to market at the point where your market has a **first** strong anchor.

MySpace was in the transformative space but not enough anchored in what people knew. Facebook when it really entered the market was already building on the customer knowledge and experience of what MySpace and others have prepared.

Ensure your products/services are as transformative as possible yet anchored in what is recognizable for your customer (TYR)

What if you have a transformational product that just is missing the anchor? Should you give up?
Of course not. What you are looking for is either to extend a previous product with an anchor or wait for other companies to work towards your product. Have you ever seen products that at launch looked like a stupid idea but that a few years later become an anchor for something great?
Look at the evolution of iTunes. Being forced to use iTunes with account etc. to copy music on your device, but with the extension of the music store and opportunity to buy individual songs rather than full albums, it is growing into a larger and larger platform while improving customer experience.

Let me clarify one more point on the anchors.
They can be technological, emotional, environmental, or knowledge based.
The coronavirus is one of the most impactful events. Schools closing, borders closing, restaurants dying, and an increase in home office activities of 50%. Thousands of new anchors are being established due to this which will create new beliefs. Anyone who will come with a better version of toilet paper or even one of the Asian water-based cleaning toilets will be able

to exploit the experience many had during the supermarket's food and toilet paper shortages.

This principle can also be used in product design. A short while back a start-up came to me asking for advice on their algorithm. A pre-revenue start-up with a focus on recommending your next day trip or your next destination based on where your friends have gone. During the discussion, we discussed how we can use a KNN(we cover that later, not important for now) or a twin model as well as how to approach the building of the algorithm, which language and which software in their case made the most sense.
The part that was most exciting to them was the TYR concept as part of their recommendations.
During the discussion and through examples we looked at the different extremes.

Let us look from the customer perspective on the day trip recommendations that you might get in the app.

If we recommend to the customer only things that are exactly like where they went in the past it might become boring and reduce the times' customers will come back to the app.
If we recommend only new or transformative destinations it will feel out of place.
Thus, we took, as a rule, to ensure that at least 20% of what we recommend is in the other extreme.
For customers where we want to recommend innovative places, we will keep 20% of similar places as anchors in the recommendations.
For customers where we recommend 80% destinations they might know / or their friends know we want to mix in 20% of completely new or different destinations.

An algorithm that you are building should be built on mathematical science mixed with human or economic psychology.

As a company, you want to signal that we know you as the customer, that we understand what you want, yet that we have some other proposals as well that could make your life even more exciting.

Use TYR to test the boundaries of your products and features.

Perspective

No two persons ever have the same impression of the event.
Is the glass half-full or half-empty? A constant discussion. Early in my career, I learned that shifting viewpoints and changing your perspective makes you more adaptable, which itself will lead to more success.
I used to think about the glass half-empty. But then I realized that the question misleads me. Why is this an either-or question? The truth is that the glass is both half-empty and half-full at the same time. Why did I need to force myself to think in only one perspective?
Next, I thought, now that I understand that both are true. Does this change how I would act about that glass?
If someone would come and offer me to fill my glass, I will take the perspective that my glass is half-empty and happily accept the offer.
If someone would come and offer me to fill my glass for 2x times what it would normally cost, I would assume the half-full stance and say, "no, but thank you I still have enough".
I realized that my options to approach every problem would widen so drastically that I had a higher chance of succeeding at any problem I was seeing.

Never waste a good crisis

Is the Corona situation a crisis? Or is it an opportunity? It is both. We cannot just act in one way. We need to look both ways on the street.

A large number of companies were in major trouble during this period. From cash flow problems to recruitment problems to supply chain issues etc.
Almost all companies I talked to, created a crisis management team. Daily updates on sales, a daily update on cash flow, and supply. Most companies that were in a good situation even were looking at CSR activities and how to help the community.

- Free products
- Extended payment terms
- Better stocking
- Production of Disinfection
- And many more

Then you had a few companies that did great during this time. The biggest difference between them and the rest was that next to a crisis board they build an opportunity board. A group of people of the company that will not look at how negatively we are affected but on how we can use this time to our advantage. How they can change a product, change ways of working or change a direction.
- A platform for scheduling appointments with your doctor quickly adopted to add telemedicine to their services
- Telecom giants adopting their service portfolio
- Restaurants switching to pure delivery and offering discounts for takeaway food when wearing masks
- Recruitment companies offering virtual recruitment events with 1000s of talents
- Companies digitalizing their sales forces, upskilling their workers and mindset

There is a joke going around:

*Who was responsible for the digital
transformation in your company?*

A) CEO

B) CIO

C) COVID-19

Crisis and desperation make some people strife in creativity while others just panic. Where I live many restaurants were closing down. Even my favorite restaurant was going out of business. Some restaurants were trying to adjust to allow take away food in their restaurant. But many soon realized that take away food is usually only 10% of the revenue of what you can normally get as a restaurant owner and that the normal way of thinking e.g. most money is earned with the drinks, not the food - is out of the window if you need to change. If you change but still cling to your previous thinking many restaurants failed. If you focus on takeout food your supply chain, ordering, even your website now matters more than ever before.

Yet some companies even re-engineered the complete restaurant experience. One restaurant company decided to use the experience of people feeling alone as an anchor and the possibility of selling wine and created a virtual dinner table. You will have the wine delivered to your door. While unpacking a connoisseur will have a video call and explain how to open the wine depending on the type, how to handle it, and what is special about it.
Dinner will be given then to a group of 4 different households all with the same menu previously delivered and during the dinner, all participants are joining into the same video session to exchange but also to have the online server explain the dishes flavors and which wine best connects to each dish.

Some companies started Kickstarter campaigns to stay alive, some sold vouchers to gain customers directly after the crisis ended. Many see only the downsides, yet the only bad thing you can do during such a crisis is to do nothing.

Every crisis is an opportunity. Look at the companies that were founded during recessions:

General Electric 1892, General Motors 1908, IBM 1911, Disney 1929, HP 1939. Hyatt 1957, FedEx 1971, Microsoft 1975, EA 1982, Apple 2001, Airbnb 2008, Uber 2009, Spotify 2008.

Corona will drive new trends, create new opportunities, and new blockbuster companies.

Every situation has many perspectives. The more perspectives you can see the wider your possible tool kit of striving in change becomes.

No problem has only one perspective. Understand that the glass is both half-full as well as half-empty and adapt according to your opportunities. It is a first building block for becoming agile and a first building block to managing transformation

---

Truth

One of the most commonly spoken lies:

„I swear to speak the truth and nothing but the truth ".

Not because most people purposely lie in the court of law but because the concept of truth is a problem. In business, we often talk about the single version of the truth when it comes to data storage systems without duplications or multiple data storage. A single place where the "true" numbers are visible. Unfortunately, this is largely an illusion – in both business as well as life.

Please entertain the idea that there are 3 types of truth:
- the personal truth
- the objective truth
- the evolving truth

The personal truth is your truth. It is what you believe and based on your experiences and your interpretation of the world. It is also the truth that is most impacted by millions of biases you have.

- Is 30.000 USD for a Tesla a fair price?
- In the last argument with your wife/husband, who was right and who was wrong?
- Are 25 degrees too warm?
- Is AI going to change the world?
- Should you change your job?
- Does God exist?

Your personal beliefs will answer 80% of these questions supported by 20% of objectives facts, which your mind carefully sub-selects to reinforce your thinking. You will answer the questions mostly driven by how the question makes you feel and if you can connect it to something you experienced.

Take the example of some doomsday cults. A few years back when such a cult reached the day of reckoning and was supposed to kill themselves to be liberated and to ascend only to be stopped by the police in time. A day later when the day of reckoning did not come, the cult members were asked how they felt about this. Their personal truth was that the doomsday was prevented because they tried to act according to their beliefs. Personal truth is about how we as individuals color the facts around us.

The objective truth is about facts and scientific data evaluation. You are reading this text right now. That is a fact. I cannot tell if you like it or hate it. It is fact that outside it is 25 degrees Celsius. We can calculate it and it is true no matter whom you ask.

One key aspect of data science which as a key part of digital transformation we will dive in a bit later is to improve the objective truth. Yet to be clear data science & AI are very far from the objective truth.

The goal is not to be right, but to be less wrong

Look at the truth like a game of "Battleship".

Two players have a fleet of ships. No player knows the other's ship's positions. One after another you shoot on individual fields on a 10 x 10 grid.

The objective truth is where exactly each ship is located and if you would reveal all pieces to both players there would be no dispute on where they are positioned. Yet like in life you are in a situation of limited information or an asynchronous information environment. You do have a personal truth of where you believe the opponent's ships to be located and thus you "shoot" at fields you believe in. Sometimes you hit. Sometimes you miss it.

Over time your perceived personal picture of the truth shapes. Creating an evolving reality. What you believed to be true can change drastically with a single piece of new information. This is the evolving truth.

The closer you are to the objective truth the better decision you will take. Data science or augmented decision making is about taking the data to transform your personal truth and move it closer to the objective truth by including new types of data in like how does the last hit change the probability of each ship's position. Can you read your opponent? Are they more likely to place ships in the corners or the middle? How have they played the last time?
Business relies largely on taking the right decisions at the right time, which in turn requires a more and more close connection to the objective truth.

In business, you are not playing a finite game and will never reach a state of complete objective truth. You might understand what someone has done but like in the game you will never fully understand why they have done what they did. In business decision making you will need to reach a state in which you use analytics/AI/data to get closer to the objective truth, knowing that **your goal is not to be right, but your goal is to be less wrong**.

Assume everyone including you is wrong.

Recognize your goal is not to be right but less wrong.

Realize that achieving a complete objective truth in business is almost impossible. Use data and facts to complement your thinking and challenge your own biases

As humans, we are ultimately always receptive to storytellers that challenge.

Let me tell you two stories:

We analyzed the sumo sport. Sport in the last 20 years has often been framed as increasingly fraudulent. The Russian doping scandal, boxers throwing games, tour de France doping, Belgium soccer league players manipulating games, and many more. Mark Grace once said: If you are not cheating you are not trying. So, let's use data to tell a story. We took the official match results between 1989 and 200 with around 32,000 bouts fought over 200 wrestlers. Now in sumo ranking is everything. It determines your salary, your food, how much you get to sleep, and which chores you have to do in your sumo stable. The lowest ranking sumo will need to wash their superiors and show respect whenever required. The top 66 wrestlers are grouped in the so-called makuuchi and juryo divisions. The sumo	We analyzed the sumo sport. Sport is about motivation. As in companies' incentive schemes are truly changing behaviors. Many of us know the stories of the honorable samurai and the bushido code of Japanese society. Let us use data on how incentive schemes can have people reach new heights. We took the official match results between 1989 and 200 with around 32,000 bouts fought over 200 wrestlers. Now in sumo ranking is everything. It determines your salary, your food, how much you get to sleep, and which chores you have to do in your sumo stable. The lowest ranking sumo will need to wash their superiors and show respect whenever required. The top 66 wrestlers are grouped in the so-called makuuchi and juryo divisions. The sumo world is split into the east and the west.

world is split into the east and the west.

The ranking is defined as the results of the six tournaments in which each fighter has a total of 15 fights (each time one fight per day). If you have 8 or more wins, thus more wins than loses, you will raise in the ranking. Otherwise, you will fall. Thus your 8th win is critical to push you in the right ranking level. So, let us look at the last day of the tournament and evaluate matches where a 7-7 fighter fights an 8-6 fighter. Considering that both have comparable results in this tournament the probability of the 7-7 fighter to win should be around 49-50%. Yet if you look in the data the actual win % for the 7-7 fighter was 80%. When they fought the same opponents in other tournaments without the pressure and the incentive to win their win ratio was only 50%.

The only times where the actual percentage was around 50% was shortly after allegations have been made that certain fighters were rigging the game.

The ranking is defined as the results of the six tournaments in which each fighter has a total of 15 fights (each time one fight per day). If you have 8 or more wins, thus more wins than loses, you will raise in the ranking. Otherwise, you will fall. Thus your 8th win is critical to push you in the right ranking level. So, let us look at the last day of the tournament and evaluate matches where a 7-7 fighter fights an 8-6 fighter. Considering that both have comparable results in this tournament the probability of the 7-7 fighter to win should be around 49-50%. Yet if you look in the data the actual win % for the 7-7 fighter was 80%. Pushed with the motivation to not fall in the ranking it catapulted their skills to a new level. Imagine how you can use such incentives to drive your employee's motivation. When they fought the same opponents in other tournaments without the pressure and the incentive to win their win ratio was only 50%.

Proving most sports are fraudulent.	Take an example of the sumo fighters putting everything on the line in one of the most honor-bound societies of the world and see how incentives can drive performance.

Does the story seem true to you?

When testing individuals to read randomly one of the stories 78% agreed that what was said is sound and true (the truth). After reading both stories this % dropped to 55%. Showing how susceptible we are to storytelling. And that truth is not always the objective truth. In business, decision making, & analytics we want to drive the objective truth, which means that each problem needs to be analyzed from very different angles. Being a great digital leader means that while we must be good at telling stories we must be better at identifying a story to manage our truth.

Being a great digital leader means that while we must be good at telling stories we must be better at identifying fake stories

Digital Change

Can change be managed? How to direct and structure change? How to manage change? Deep questions that whole books have been written about, studies published, and opinions formed.

Change management in its purest form is the orchestration of the transition between the status quo and a newly designed end state by guiding the journey of people, processes, organizations & technologies. In projects today we do a great job at managing the technology implementation & the process/ governance changes, but we often completely underestimate the people, organizational & perception side of change. Far too often I have seen a project that has great project plans, a well-defined critical path, waterfall or agile coaches, and project management on a very sophisticated level fail.

When we look at change management in these projects you usually see three different variations
- No change management whatsoever
- Change management is indicated as a continuous line without milestone or specific activities
- Change management is only placed at the end of the project plan and contains a few pieces of training & bits of communication.

Change is hard. In many ways it might be the hardest activity at work you can imagine. I often hear that people do not like change as an excuse for why change management is failing. We should probably tell that to the fashion industry that people don't like changing cloth and want new designs. We should probably tell Apple that no one needs their new inventions. We should probably tell the travel industry that no one likes changing locations. Change is something beautiful in our lives. Think about your friends when they start a new job on how much they shine. Think about people who want to change and start running marathons, on how much excitement they spread.

And now think about the last transformations in your company. Barely anyone is excited about it. Far the opposite. You feel an animosity & sometimes hate towards the thoughts on it. Of course, also in private life, the change is often hard, but you still hear positivity surrounding it. Barely any company manages that people talk about their transformation positively. So why is change within our companies so hard.

7 Reasons change is hard in companies
1) Change Fatigue
Probably the biggest reason first. We often forget the amount of change that is going on each day for every given individual. At work and in private. In our projects and change management, we often act as if the projects stand alone. "Oh, we only need to train the sales reps on this for 8 hours. They should easily be able to free 8 hours for something this important." Yet 10 projects are going on at the same time which all have the same thought. Remember the project is never as important for them as you think it is for you.

In one roadmap design workshop, we looked at what projects we run in the next 6 months. At the end of the meeting, almost everyone felt happy and each project believed it can be handled. Until we did one small test by crossing how many projects will "hit" the same stakeholders at the same time. The result was:

"We are planning to change whom the sales reps target when they talk to the customer, we ask them to switch from Face to Face meetings to largely digital interaction, we implement a new CRM system that they need to enter their information and we switch their cars to full electric. And by the way, they need to sell a new product. Do we believe anyone can handle this effectively?". Which sounds like a joke, is the reality in 90% of companies I talked to. Life is complex and so is the life of a company. Employees will choose certain changes and will drop others. We all have a certain change capacity of what you can handle in terms of your change resilience. Some more and some less but there is a limit. I once heard the saying that you are either in a change, going into a change, or coming out of a change. The truth might be more like that at the same time we are in 10 changes before, during, and after them.

In business, we talk about focus and about what our priorities are. Change capacity is not infinite, handle it as a resource that you can spend but you better spend it well.

2) Fake News Fake Change

We often hear the topic of fake news today. Incorrect information spread and unnecessary attention paid to it. Conspiracy theories, political opinion building, and much wasted time. Fake change is a long-lasting symptom in companies. How often have we announced fake change? Maybe we even went through a reorganization or a new product feature implementation and nothing has, in reality, has changed. Moreover, none cared. We talk so much about change that sometimes we do not even realize our change is not even real.

3) Change via 1 message

At a company seminar, I loved a statement and that influenced my way of thinking drastically. It was that everything starts with why.
That you want to engage people with why we are here? Why are we doing this? And that we want to spend less time on what and how, but more on the why. So, I started presenting my projects always with why. I thought I was so great. Only later it hit me that out of the 10 people in the room there might have been only two that were moved by the why. "My" why. At that

point, I realized, that you always start with the why but that why might be 10 things to 10 people.

When we bring messages, we need to ensure to broaden why to cover multiple small variations of your story as people will be influenced by slightly different people. I do believe it is meanwhile impossible to create a universal true mission statement.

I saw that some people were motivated by creating the best product, others by leading the industry, others by the innovation, and others by the artistic design of the product. When bringing the why of your story please create a concise statement that still covers the key drivers of your audience.

Key prerequisite: You need to know your audience.

4) Missing positivity

We learn through positivity. Enjoy through positivity. We only achieve our best when we are positive. It is even medically proven that positivity is healing your body. That is why we placebo test in medicine and we see how the body cures cancer or other diseases without medical treatment.

Yet in company changes, positivity is the last thing we count on. We people come back home from work and complain. We often soothe our worries by complaining. Trying to get support and complain or gossip about how hard life is.

If you want lasting change, we need to create a spirit of positivity. Which sounds like an easy thing to do, but it is far from it. Good news travels slow, bad news travels fast. This means we need to over-communicate and create twice as much good news as bad news is surrounding us.

We are better to celebrate outward successes than inward. Change happens from within. In ourselves but also our organization. We can never change the perception of the customer if we cannot change the perception within our teams.

5) Believing a good purpose is enough for people changing

Humans are egoists and self-centered. A purpose is great but not enough to fully convince people about change. Many projects, even if they had a great purpose were not able to build engagement in the company - otherwise, healthcare companies would be the most progressively changing companies in the world.

6) No investment in building adaptable resilience

The survival of the fittest

Darwin most quoted idea and worldwide known. Sadly, it is the most misinterpreted one. It is often considered as the survival of the strongest, yet the actual meaning was the survival of the most adaptable. It is not about being the strong man/woman but that in times of need we adapt to what is necessary. In evolution, we must adjust to so many different situations & external influences. We adjust our food according to the circumstances. We adjust our cloth. We adjust our lifestyle. We adapt to the culture around us. Even our human features from the form of your eyes to our arms and legs have adapted to the environment.

You see it in nature everywhere including extreme examples like chameleons that are adapting literally to their background. Resilience and adaptability are skills of the same spectrum but different ends. We need resilience to not get lost in all the changes we have around us and sometimes withstand the unnecessary or negative changes coming our way. Adaptability means we need to adjust our ways of working and to graph opportunities when we see it and jump on the change trains that lead to a new world of positive changes.

Communication, training, and workshops can help prepare the employees on all the journeys around them. Teach your team how to manage their energy. Changes are exhausting but with better foundations and capabilities in resilience and adaptability, you can amplify the change impact positively.

7) Missing Accountability & Commitment

Upon a very recent IBM survey, 65% of CFOs believe that applying advanced analytics and AI within finance is very important to their strategy, yet only 1 on 5 has experienced it in the last 12 months.

I cannot tell if this is a new change that has transitioned over many years or if it was a problem that was always there. Looking at many companies and projects there is such a lack of commitment, a lack of the will to start & accountability to see things through to the end. Maybe it is culture, maybe we just had too good lives. Maybe the change was not needed at such a high speed.

While I always understood that consultants will leave at the end of the project and will have little (self)interest in long term successful solutions, the same syndrome has been observed in internal projects as well. There always seemed to be a disconnect between the project teams & the internal or external customers. Teams usually got rewarded for executing projects, not for executing change that leads to impact. Partially, because the bonus payments are yearly, and impact is hard to measure yearly but might need multiple years to reach fulfillment.

We will need to adjust our rewards & other recognition factors to make sure we reward commitment, and we make people accountable for the results.

7 most common misunderstanding about Change management

Misunderstanding 1: Change management is the role of the Change Manager

If you believe your change manager is the only accountable for the change management, you will have a nasty surprise at the end of your project. Change is universal accountability of the complete project team, the complete management & your customers. The role of a change manager or change catalyst or change agent or change conductor is the orchestrate the change transition. To make sure the right pieces are in play, the planning is done & perfectly executed. Yet the convincing the communication, the sharing, and engagement will need to come from the complete team. This also means that sometimes you need to get your best developer out of the project if their negativity is spreading outside the project team. Only if the whole team moves in the same direction you can enable the best possible change transition.

Misunderstanding 2: Change management = Communication & Training

If your change management consists only of communication & training, you have misunderstood the concept. Let me take you through a company example who has built an amazing solution yet shot themselves in the back by misunderstanding change management. The company builds an amazing solution to improve its sales force targeting by using the next best action AI. Basically, recommending to the Sales Reps what is the next best action to take. A customer has opened an email or clicked on your website on a certain product and the AI automatically recommends visiting the customer today and help them with their questions. The expectation was to increase sales by 20%

in the areas where this was going to be effective. The solution worked well, the right level of recommendations & great speed. Management loved the idea.

The end of the project comes, and it reaches the stage to get the sales reps instructed into how the solution work and how it helps the company. It was an 8-hour event about the logic of the technology, how it works, what they should do it, and how it will be better for the company. The result = No sales reps followed the instruction. In interviews later a few points came out:

- Sales Reps have been doing their job in a current way for an average of 10 years and we expect them to change this completely based on an 8-hour meeting. It might have been a long project. But in the eyes of the sales reps, the complete transition period of the change is 8 hours
- If they fail due to a bad recommendation - they get punished. Their bonus is based on their sales target, which means if they try and fail, they get a lower bonus (and not the project team of the AI).
- The feeling of complete loss of control. There was an enormous feeling of losing control and subsequently to lose a level of self-worth. Suddenly they were not in a position where they can choose any more what to do.

How could they have adjusted it in this case:
- Have multiple session of multiple months to start the transition in this activity
- Adjust the compensation scheme including a bonus for using the application and in case of bad recommendation a bonus compensation. If you are confident in the solution, you can put money where your mouth is
- Add an additional level of accountability for the project team. Their bonus should be linked to the sales rep's performance after using the application. Too often

project teams have a disconnected performance measurement, where they get rewarded for project completion disregarding the eventual impact

- Allow a certain degree of freedom in choosing and providing a feedback loop towards the AI to improve recommendations

Change Management is a combination of processes, incentive schemes, Accountability, communication, the building of competency, engagement, mindset & behavioral influencing, marketing. Only when we approach all of them holistically can change flourish and then the transition can become exciting rather than painful.

Misunderstanding 3: Change management is a small part of the project

Change management is a massive effort. As a simple rule, you need to spend usually 2x the amount of work on change management than you need to spend on individual project implementation time.

Misunderstanding 4: If someone is asking for your project, change management is easier

During my first projects in AI / Digital, I was believing that if my customer is asking for a project or ask me first insights on a specific business question that it will make my job easier and change management less important.
Oh, I was so wrong on this...
I did exactly answer the question they were looking for and was completely caught off guard. It felt surreal at that point to me but looking back the fault was mine. I realized that the same was true in my private life. Only because someone wants to lose weight and want to know how to do, does not mean they will like the answer.

In the future I learned that I needed to start each project with change management no matter who is asking for it, the effort is always there.

Misunderstanding 5: Change management starts at the end of your project

---

Change management is NOT PART of project management

Project management is PART of change management

Change management by far transcends the project management in terms of timelines, relevance, and impact in my eyes. Change management starts long before your project starts and long after it completes. Project management is to transition the creation/change of technologies, product development, etc from start to end on time, on budget, on the scope. Change management is about managing the change from the status quo to a new end-state, which includes all types of change including the technology/project elements as well as all human & psychology elements. Change management starts with even selecting the right projects to run, the people to staff in the projects, the right business question/problems to tackle and it ends with people having completely and utterly emerged themselves in a new way of working. Change management often runs over many different projects or even programs.

Misunderstanding 6: Change management profiles are hard to find

Companies often ignore 1 key department when staffing change management profiles: Their own marketing teams. Their only job is the "change/transition" the perception of their customers from one place to the other. Use these profiles also internally. They have a clear change they want to create and will use multiple projects to reach that goal.

Misunderstanding 7: Change management is top-down

Top-down change management is a split issue. On the one hand, if you do not have top management support in your change it is making a transition a lot harder. On the other hand, if you have top-down support it does not guarantee buy-in from the rest of the organization unless you work in a dictatorship. Change is covering the complete organization (or target group) and needs to cover all hierarchy levels. It will depend on the organizational culture if top-down or bottom-up or via change hotspots in the center will be most effective.

The rules of the game

Your cards

We are now at the stage where we can add the meaning behind some of the most used buzz words and how they interact, even if it might not be their definition. I don't believe that you need to understand the combustion engine of a car even if you are a car driver but that rather you understand the logic on which it is built and how to use it. Let us start with a few short interpretations of individual words and how I will be looking at them in this book.

Digital the most common usage of the word digital is when it is encompassing technology that converts the "real world" into data and uses this data to generate real-world value for individuals or companies while being in a connected environment. This means it includes AI, Omnichannel marketing, data warehouses, Voice-over-IP (like Skype), web conferencing, blockchain, social media, electronic payments and electronic currencies like Apple Pay, websites, self-driving cars, online marketplaces like Amazon and eBay, AR, VR and the internet of things. This broad definition is one of the reasons why digital is often misunderstood and disconnected from the business. The most important point is that as a business your strategy needs to be digital, you should never have a separate digital strategy. If you have a separate department working on "digital strategy" next to your core, you are probably only getting 10% of what you could get out of your activities.

Your customer today is digital. There is no question if you should go digital, there is only the question, when will you be how much digital.

In many job interviews, I asked people for their interpretation of digital business. You will have two types of answers:

- Making our processes and ways of working more efficient and effective due to digital automation
- Generate new value propositions revenue streams or unlock existing product potential using digital technologies

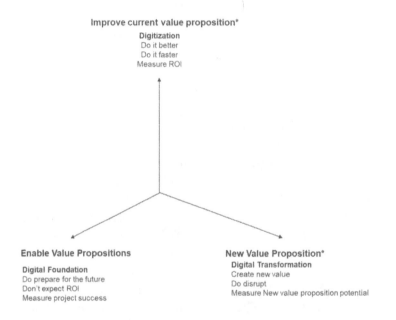

Improve current value proposition*
Digitization
Do it better
Do it faster
Measure ROI

Enable Value Propositions
Digital Foundation
Do prepare for the future
Don't expect ROI
Measure project success

New Value Proposition*
Digital Transformation
Create new value
Do disrupt
Measure New value proposition potential

When I hire people, this was one of the key questions where both options are right, but none is complete. Only if you understand that there are three axes of digital, you will understand the complexity of digital. All projects even if they are all part of the digital family require three very distinctly different altitudes of change management, project management, and portfolio management.

Therefore we must consider 3 areas of digital

- **Digitalization**: This is the improvement of an existing value proposition by using digital means especially through effectiveness, agility, quality, and efficiency gain. The simplest example is if a brick and mortar chain is implementing electronic invoicing & an inventory system to accelerate the administration of payments and stock overview.

- **Digital transformation**: This is the creation of a new value proposition using digital with new business models often generating new revenue streams or disruptively improving one's value proposition.
True Digital transformation projects contrary to digitalization are concretely driving a major change in your operating model, your products, and have a concrete large-scale impact on your revenue streams and/or core activities. The simplest example is if the owner of a brick and mortar chain is adjusting its business model and is creating an online store. Just remember that transformation is about people thus it can be about your customer or your employees.

- **Digital foundation**: This is the building of foundations and capabilities that are required in the future to improve existing or create new value propositions. They are needed often forgotten as they do not have a direct ROI and are not as business sexy. The simplest example is when a store upscales its employees on digital capabilities and builds a database with easy access to data.

7 key aspects to understand about Digitalisation

1) The key goal is:

Improve the existing value proposition. You try to do things faster, better, more efficiently, more effectively. It usually includes automation, augmented decision making, workflow optimization, robotics, and others.

2) Examples

Novartis Annual Report:
"One area is how we prepare and use marketing materials across the company, a complex process that involves about 17 000 employees globally in some way. We are shifting from a fragmented approach to a common enterprise-wide one for sharing advertisements, videos, and other marketing materials for key products among marketing teams at the global, regional, and local levels. We are creating a central digital repository for these materials so that they can be repurposed and reused globally. We anticipate this effort will save about USD 130 million over five years and reduce by 5–13% the time some employees spend creating and managing marketing materials."

BMW Group Annual Report:
"Its production network leverages innovative technologies from the fields of digitalization and Industry 4.0, including applications from the worlds of virtual reality, artificial intelligence, and 3D printing. Standardized processes and structures ensure consistent premium quality throughout the production system. At the same time, the BMW Group offers its customers a high degree of individualisation"

Nestle Annual Report:
"Digitalization is vital for Nestlé's continued evolution. It covers all aspects of our business, from the way we organize internally to how we engage externally. We are advancing as a digitally enabled and data powered business. Our digital journey is business-led and focused on becoming faster, more agile and more consumer-centric. We look for ways

to evolve and use technology to accelerate innovation, fuel new growth opportunities and create efficiencies. This includes using analytics, automation, artificial intelligence, and machine learning, as well as e-business (digital marketing and e-commerce). In 2019, our e-commerce sales accounted for 8.5% of sales and grew by 18.5%. This puts Nestlé at the high end of the food and beverage industry. To win in a connected world, we focus our digitalization efforts on: – Better understanding and engagement with consumers. – Enabling digital innovation and new business models. – Digitalizing our operations. – Raising digital competencies
[...]
Digitalizing our operations, We are transforming our operations by digitalizing our supply chains and manufacturing. Our goal is to create competitive gaps through data, artificial intelligence, automation, and predictive analytics. In many facilities, we are scaling up the Internet of Things with remote-sensing technologies and deploying autonomous vehicles and collaborative robots. For example, at the end of 2019: – 100 of our factories were equipped with collaborative robots. – 60 of our warehouses were automated. – 100 of our factories were paperless. Digitalization helps us generate efficiencies, create agility, and provide new platforms for growth. The shift toward agile manufacturing also helps to deliver faster innovation and supports personalization"

3) Time till the first impact after projects end

For each project, it can take between 1-12 months until you can see the first concrete business impact. Should you not see the impact after 12 months there is a high chance nothing will come.

4) Key challenge:

In each digitization, you need to convince employees to change their way of working, their skillset, and their mindset.

The key issue is that you are replacing a large part of what they do. Either in terms of how they do or how much or at which quality.

In the eyes of many, you are basically telling them "you are not good enough that is why we need to change". "Your knowledge and skill are outdated" and "everything that you considered value has just been devalued as we can just automate it".
Yes, most communication approaches and most intentions are about how good digitalization will be for the employees, but people believe the above and what is more important: it is true. Anyone who believes digitization is not impacting employees' jobs or mindset specifically their self-worth and their job activities is just in denial.
Do not ever misunderstand what you are doing. You are not just bringing technology into the companies you actively attack employee's self-confidence. You often are reaching a large amount of individuals with the digitization and it created an exponentially complex communication and engagement challenge.

1st rule of all digitalization: Always consider how the end state looks like

---

Consider how jobs of individual people are impacted and how it will make your (internal)customer feel. Do a real impact assessment. In many design projects, you already work with personas (an example of a person with real attributes and real characteristics).
You will need to use the same technique to consider how the world after your digitization looks like for each employee. This is not on an aggregate level, it not about how it impacts the job

of „accountants" or „sales managers"; it is about how it will impact the jobs and lives of Jake, Jane, and Joey. The reason most change management fails in digitization projects is that you do not even know how the future looks like. You cannot manage a path to the future you imagined if you do not even know your future. Less you cannot expect it from your employees.

5) Prioritization and measurement

To select the right digitalization projects, you choose according to ROI, Risk avoidance, or other direct contribution to your existing value proposition.

6) The risk

Depending on the scale of the digitalization project the failure rate is between 40-60%.

7) Value

Most digitalization projects have an ROI of 3x to 10x. A project below that should not be considered.

7 key aspects to understand about Digital foundation

1) The key goal is:

Your digital foundation is the preparation of the future. You need to build competency, databases, technology landscapes that you will use as an accelerator, enabler, and foundation for both digitizations as well as digital transformation.

2) Examples:

BMW Group Annual Report:
"Realignment of vocational training Started in 2018, the realignment of vocational training continued to make good progress with the implementation of various strategic action packages, aimed in particular at bringing about the digital transformation of vocational training based on three pillars: modern and mobile equipment, new digital collaboration and learning platforms, and a broadly based system of talent development specifically tailored to apprentices. In addition to the basic range of skills still needed, emphasis is also being placed on promoting the acquisition of new technical and interdisciplinary expertise across 30 vocations and 17 dual courses of study. The latter were expanded to include the bachelor-degree programmes Industry 4.0 Computer Science, Artificial Intelligence and Production and Automation"

Novartis Annual Report:
"Novartis is a data powerhouse. We've collected approximately 2 million patient-years of data through our clinical trials alone. And we're taking steps to make the most of this strategic asset. In 2019, we expanded and launched major data and digital initiatives while forming new collaborations to augment our growing internal capabilities.
Data42 is a program that's laying the technical and cultural foundation for a revolution in our organization. The ambition is to change the way that we conduct drug discovery and development in this era of big data. We're integrating massive amounts of data that previously existed in silos inside and outside the company and taking a holistic look at it. The data ranges from images of cells that have been treated with different chemicals,

to blood samples from patients analysed within clinical trials. We're using machine learning and artificial intelligence to mine the integrated, anonymized data for connections and patterns that are indiscernible to the human brain. Our data scientists are building models and applications that will empower Novartis teams to ask new questions, make better predictions and save time. We can use the platform to prioritize drug targets, identify development opportunities for compounds, and more."

Nestle:
"Raising digital competencies Our people need to have the right mindset, skills and tools. We ask them to be entrepreneurial and externally focused. We also facilitate increased collaboration through internal social networks. We have created digital academies and centres of competency to accelerate our pace of digital transformation. Among them: – The Global Digital Hub in Barcelona allows us to respond to fast-paced technological changes by building expertise in areas such as artificial intelligence and cloud technologies. – The Global Digital Media Center of Competencies brings together all our advertising agencies to deliver greater efficiency and transparency in our media investments. – The Silicon Valley Innovation Outpost enables us to source new ideas and drive digital innovation with partners."

3) Time till the first impact after projects end

For each project, it can take between 6-18 months till you can see the first concrete business impact, but it requires a project utilizing the foundation with in the first 6 months of building. Otherwise, people lose interest in the foundation. To build a house 33% of the time is spent on the foundation & prework before you see anything above ground.

4) Key challenge:

The key challenge is that it is an unrewarding job. Most foundations take the longest to build and will not directly show for anything which will mean also limited recognition is shared with people working on them.

5) Prioritization and measurement

You select a project based on how strong they will support future key projects and afterward you measure success via projects success metrics & employee NPS & comparison to benchmarks

6) The risk

Depending on the scale of the foundation project the failure rate is between 20-40%.

7) Value

The overall impact on your company in successful projects is 0x. You are not creating a direct impact. You create value indirectly through better digitalization and digital transformation projects.

7 key aspects to understand about Digital Transformation

1) The key goal is:

Create a new value proposition. It usually contains disruptive elements for customers & employees including new business models and major organizational shifts.

2) Examples from annual reports

Adidas Annual Report:

"The digital transformation is fundamentally changing the way our consumers behave and the way we work. Technology has enabled us to accelerate building direct relationships with our consumers. Improving digital capabilities along the entire value chain enables us not only to interact with the consumer, but also to become faster, better, and more efficient in every part of the organization. We continue to make strong progress in multiple digital accelerators. After the initial launch in 2017, we expanded the reach of the adidas app to over 30 countries across all major markets. Our membership program Creators Club introduced in 2018 as well as the relaunch of the Runtastic app as 'adidas Running by Runtastic' and 'adidas Training by Runtastic', respectively, emphasize the importance of our investments in customer relationship management to allow a deeper consumer understanding. By providing consumers with a premium, connected, and personalized shopping experience, we progress toward our 2020 own e-commerce revenue target of € 4 billion. In 2019, our own e-commerce platform was our fastest-growing channel with a currency-neutral revenue increase of 34%."

BMW Annual Report:

"With BMW Connected and the growing digital offerings, the Company is prepared for the expectations and wishes of its customers. In this regard, the focus is not just on the development and integration of new technologies and services for the vehicle, but on customers and their

contemporary demands. Digital services, which customers are used to, should be available seamlessly and without restrictions even outside of the vehicle."

Nestle Annual Report:

"Enabling digital innovation and new business models: Nespresso's subscription service Nespresso continually evolves its digital ecosystem. The latest addition is a convenient machine and coffee subscription service for businesses and consumers. The service boosts retention by rewarding loyalty and gives users the ability to tailor purchasing plans, trial limited-edition coffees, and connect via our Internet of Things-enabled machines."

3) Time till the first impact after projects end

For each project, it can take between 12-36 months until you can see the first concrete business impact. Overall digital transformation programs take on average 7 years.

4) The main challenge is:

The key challenge is the complete holistic transformation. It cannot be handled as a disconnected technology project but as multisided change engagements. You need to approach each aspect of digital transformation individually & collectively.

5) Prioritization and measurement

You select digital transformation projects based on disruption potential (not financial ROI), strategic alignment & afterwards measure customer NPS & financial impact

6) The risk

70% of all digital transformation projects fail.

7) Value

The overall impact on your company in successful projects can be between 10x – 100x.

(Table): Digitalisation Digital Transformation Digital foundation

	Digitalisation	Digital Transformation	Digital foundation
Value Proposition focus	Improve existing	Create new	Support both
Measurement	ROI	Disruption potential & strategic alignment & customer NPS	Projects success metrics & employee NPS & benchmarks
Example brick and mortar store	implement electronic invoicing to accelerate the administration of payments and stock overview	creating an online store next to their physical store generating a new revenue stream	upscales their employees on digital capabilities and build a customer data warehouse
Change management Challenge	People afraid they lose their jobs	Requires the organization and employees to completely reinvent themself	Employees do not see the direct value for the company and do not commit
Risk Level	Low	High	Medium
Time till the first impact after projects end	1-12 month	12-36 month	6-18 month
Direct value	1.5x to 3x	10x – 100x	0x

7 reasons your digital transformation hits a wall

Amsterdam, Conference about Digital Transformation. A large number of experts are talking about their amazing digital transformation, about how they single-handed brought digital to their company. How they bought a huge cloud service. How they orchestrated some amazing apps. How many advanced analytics POCs have been finished and that they even try a blockchain development? I was flashed. I was excited. I felt depressed about how slow we are. And I was impressed by how much these experts knew. I wanted to get to know them more. How they really made this happen. How smart you must be to create such an impact.

One bottle of an amazing red wine later... the situation looked rather different. Most analytics POCs never made any impact and never moved out of the proof of concept stage. People spend millions on services, apps, and platforms that are not used. Insights provided based on wrong data. Using technologies without understanding even one bit of it.
The longer the discussion went, the more people started to remove the „pink pony "dream and shared why their digital transformation did fall flat. Out of that following, 7 misconceptions were most impactful.

Mistake 1: You think it is about the technology

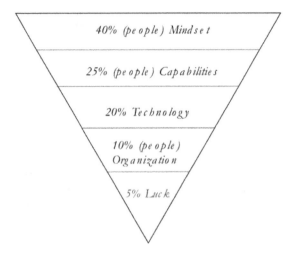

Digital Transformation is: 40% (people) Mindset, 25% (people) Capabilities, 20% Technology, 10% (people) Organization & Governance, 5% Luck.

Everyone who starts a digital transformation from a tool/technology angle will fail. If you set out to build a solution by using e.g. blockchain then work towards finding the problem, it is the perfect predictor for failure. And I do not mean the "I learn from failure so let's try"; I mean the "I wasted time and burned money while I could have known better" type of failure.

Digital in every aspect a people topic. Especially digital transformation is 75% a people/ mindset / culture problem.

If you ever implemented a solution that no one adopted, or an app that was also most never downloaded or a platform you decommissioned, you will recognize the fact that you started from the technology, not the problem and not the people.

Digital transformation means you need to work holistically on mindset changes, employee competencies, customer awareness, partner collaborations, digital knowledge, incentive schemes, and solution-finding techniques.

Most technologies are old. Nothing would have prevented you 15 years ago to build AI, blockchains, robotics, or other digital solutions. Even SAP has a speech recognition software embedded in its ERP for over 12 years (but no one used it). You will always need to have 3 key components.

The **right focus on people** (organization, competency, and mindset) the **right problem** to solve, and the **right technology**.

- People + Problem - Technology = you solve the right problem with the right people with an outdated technology

- Technology + Problem - People = you have a vision but cannot implement it or you have a solution that no one uses

- People + Technology - Problem = you build a great solution that no one needs but you might get a positive result – But you can write a nice whitepaper

- People + Problem + Technology = success

Mistake 2: You allow negativity to spread

Employees are humans (not in the sense of Human Resources but in the real sense of having emotions and needs). In a transformation, there is nothing more effective than positivity and nothing more destructive than negativity. Change that is done in an environment of negativity is born out of fear. People will work against you on so many levels and even your best project member will work in constant depression. You need to build positivity in your behavior, in your leadership, any communication is done. The greatest projects that would have helped people strive, will fail due to succumbing to negativity.

What to do: Celebrate again and again. Congratulations for every success. Control the story by ensuring from day one you know how the communications should flow. And remove negative people from your project.

A complaining person will spread like cancer and infect others. It might not be pretty but sometimes you need to lose some things to allow the future to unfold.

Mistake 3: Your travel budget is higher than your training budget

A great indicator if you are serious about transformation is if you invest in people. Look into your cost reports. If your travel budget or license budget is higher than your training budget, you are preventing your own foundations to be built.

Mistake 4: You hire young people only because you believe they are digital

There was a great DreamReachMedia spot that liked to emphasize the point that digital natives are not necessarily business digital natives. It was the setting of an interview at a prestigious company for an entry-level position.

The interviewer at one point starts asking "You mentioned in your CV that you know digital technologies. That is truly a great asset. Let us go into the details. Do you know PowerPoint"?
"No".
"Do you know excel?"
"No".
"Publisher or website creators"
"Not really"
Bewildered the interviewer stared correcting his glasses.
"In what area of technology are you an expert?"

"Snapchat, Pinterest, Vine, TikTok, Twitter - the big ones," the *interviewee said with full enthusiasm!*
"I am surprised you didn't say Facebook"
Both laugh out loud.
"That's for old people like my parents"

"The position you applied to is a research position. This means that you will need to go through a lot of information, aggregate, and summarize to send it to me."
"For stuff like that no problem: I just ask Siri or Google"
"Tell Siri that I want you to be at work at 8:00 each day"
"I don't understand "
"Which part?"
"8:00 like in the morning"
"Why? "
"8:00 does not work for me. Who gets up at 8:00. I skype with my friends till 3 am and I cannot even get to Starbucks before 10. I work best in the morning at 10:45."
"We are not going to be a good fit I believe"
"Why are you so negative," the candidate says flabbergasted.
"I can sense your hostilities and I am not feeling very safe here in this situation. I have been here for 5 min and the only nice thing you have said to me was a nice resume, which I typed ALL night for this meeting. You have given me no guidance, no validation, no encouragement, no supervision. Is there an HR director I can talk to?"
"No."

It was a great video covering many millennial clichés. A bit over the top for sure but true at heart. In 2018 there was another story that schools had to replace analog clocks with digital ones as it was too hard for many to read the time and estimate how much time was left till the end of their exams. The clocks were never replaced (probably for cost reasons) but the core message still stands.
Being born a digital native does not mean you are natively good at digital.

Yet do not get me wrong. Millennials are not part of a bad generation. Just don't confuse a generation with the capability that individual people have. For any generation to succeed the right environment needs to be created.

Mistake 5: You do not hire young people because of lacking experience

You want to transform and create something new, yet you look for people who are experienced in the area you are going to.
It is oxymoronic to believe such employees exist.
In new technologies like "blockchain" or "AI," 3 years of experience make you a senior.
Your new employees have their greatest asset in having no experience - use it. They will not be locked down by a historic thinking of it "has always been like this".

Mistake 6: You think too short term

If you work on transformation and you have a 6-month plan on how to achieve it - you are either the least ambitious or the most optimistic company that exists. Changing people is a hard road. Your transformation plans should be looking out for the next 3 years minimum. Not just because you will really need this time but also because it creates a digital vision that creates excitement for your employees.

Mistake 7: Your leader is not digital

I do not believe that transformation starts at the top. I believe transformation starts with oneself, but it can get derailed from the top. A leader that is digital is the highest success criteria I know, yet that does not mean the person has any technical skills. It is about supporting the digital vision and letting more qualified people handle the rest.

(Tactic) Circular digital portfolio

Digital in business cannot succeed if we do not manage it holistically and without planning. A key in succession planning is to build a combined portfolio covering the three axes of digital.
What is the right size for your portfolio?

A garden is only complete when there is nothing more that can be removed

---

It means that we want to have a balanced portfolio of foundations, transformation, and digitalization but without any unnecessary projects. Circular digital is an aspect that you want to consider when doing your roadmap, investment, and strategic planning exercises. Many companies struggle to evaluate what is the right balance between any of the three project value types above. Some companies hope for massive digitalization projects without having any foundations. How successful you think the many companies that are trying to reinvent themselves with AI, but never implemented a single data warehouse and never trained their employees to work with AI. Some other companies invest heavily in digitalization missing long term opportunities.

The best ratio which is called circular digital is that the ROI of your digitization projects should fund your digital foundation efforts and your transformation ambitions. Use this ratio when not sure about your investment strategy unless you are in crisis mode. To check the health of your portfolio always check if the sum of ROI is covering your overall total investments.

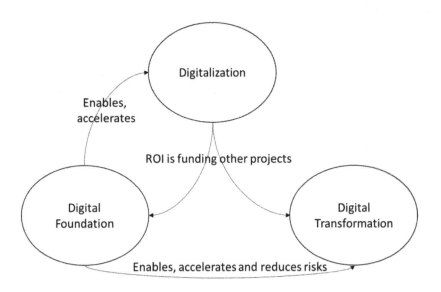

This idea born out of the initial idea of self-funding once's digital efforts is both the most balanced and risk-adjusted distribution as well as ensuring commitments of individual project leaders. Ensuring that each project understands that is vital for the organization as being a part in a circular portfolio.

Decision making has gone digital

The quality of decisions is like the well-timed swoop of a falcon which enables it to strike and destroy its victim - Sun Tsu

---

Coming back from the conference I was both happy that what we are doing is not so far behind what others are doing as well as utterly depressed. Depressed about how little expert groups know and how much expertise is bluffing. By no means, I am feeling I know a lot, but I realized that I might be looking at the problem the wrong way. Rather than looking at finding conferences that talked about how great they are executing their projects and how "innovative" their "innovations" are, I would start looking at **what did not work**. So, my next conference I went to was one of these "Fuck up conferences". Conferences dedicated to how badly each of the projects messed up. No hidden tricks, just purely the part that hurt their projects.

I was lucky to have found that the conference not only was it having the right format but also one of the sexiest Digital topics in 2019: Artificial Intelligence.

Now growing up in the last century I would have never thought data science or programming to become sexy. But I was dead wrong.

Data science is in theory the skill to combine, enrich, analyze Data via statistical models, and derive insights to inform decisions. It is used anywhere you can think of.

Which movie gets proposed to you by Netflix is based on an AI algorithm. The weather forecast = AI. Your credit rating. Fraudulent detection and many more. Even which ads are shown to you. And under the promise that data is your greatest resource, and every company is basically sitting on a pot of gold, you will find a surge in AI. A huge amount of open data science positions, the fact that "data sciences" are the best-rated jobs in the world, MBA of Data science, schools specialized in data science basically everything short of artificial intelligence merchandising is booming.

I have already used the word AI, Data Science and Analytics on the first few pages probably 20 times. Which is probably at the low end of the ratio of how the word is used in today's media or by companies.

Let us start with a few definitions. Most common definitions start from what are the parts of AI.

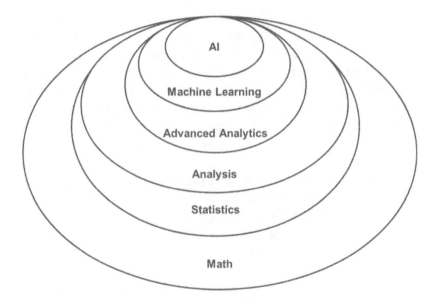

- It starts with mathematics as the core element.
- Statistics is built on top of it.
- followed by analysis,
- followed by advanced analytics,

- followed by machine learning,
- followed by AI.

You cannot have AI without machine learning. You cannot have machine learning without statistics. You cannot have statistics without mathematics. The in the reverse is not true. You can have machine learning without AI. You can have statistics without machine learning. You can have math without statistics.

- AI or artificial intelligence is a product using self-learning (machine learning) from data to solve a given problem. The learning can be enabled through pure data learning or through feedback loops and does not require manual coding or rule updates to adapt to a given situation.

- Machine learning is a set of algorithms that can learn from data and build models largely without human input or with the human only in a supervising role.

- Analytics is the toolbox of techniques that are used to take data, build models (that mostly represent a problem in the real world), and inform a decision / solve a problem.

While the above helps in framing and the definition, I prefer to look at AI from the lens of the user rather than the lens of technology. How does this look like in an example?

Please finish the following number chain

2 4 8 16 32 ...
3 6 12 24 48 ...
5 10 20 40 80 ...

I guess you were able to guess 64, 96, and 160 rather easily. What you basically did is use the past data and make a prediction. Machine learning is doing the same. It would look for patterns based on the data points and try to build a model that fits and then project it further. The difference to traditional programming is that you would do that without telling the system that the formula behind is new value = last value x 2.

Please finish the following number chain
8 ...

Most likely your first idea based on your recent experience is that it would be 16.
Unconsciously your brain has built a model that could fit and solve the above challenge. Practically it could be any number possible but if you had to decide you would choose 16. Considering all the information you had this is the best decision you could have done. This transversal thinking is one key ability that made humans the most intelligent species that ever existed on this earth.
This ability separates the micro-level machine learning from macro-level machine learning that we will look at a later stage.

Is it not ironic how we tell ourselves that we need to know everything, and we need all the facts? We know we will never have all the facts, yet we insist on it. In a business environment, you encounter the "100%" mentality, the need to know things to 100% to make a decision, which seems like a great yet never realizable ambition.

Can you tell me what the below words are?

- Ktchn
- Knfe
- Frk
- Frdg

\- Bttle

Even without something that is key in the English language such as vocals, you still understand exactly what this was about (or at least 80%). The last word could have been Bottle, Battle, Bittle, or Buttle, yet considering context, we can guess it's the first one. The same way we need to think when preparing decisions, we need the right key information, but we do not need 100% to take a direction. Take the 70/40 model.

It basically says never to take a decision when you have less than 40% of the information even if your gut tells you to, as the probability of unnecessary failure is way too high.
If you make a decision with more than 70% of the information, you are going to act too late.
If I give you the lottery number for the next weeks at 50% probability it is going to be very valuable for you. If I give 100% correctly the lottery numbers of last week, you do not gain a lot.
Business and digital decision-making are speed and the ability to make decisions at the right time. **Get used to getting it wrong**. You need to get to know when to hedge your bets, when to fold, and when to just hold your breath and see how things play out. Unfortunately, you will always see companies instead discuss watermelon KPI; **outside green inside red**. Discussing numbers for the sake of numbers.
Yet not taking a decision is always a decision for the status quo. Inaction is an action that reinforces what you do today, don't ever believe that waiting is without consequences.

In business as in life, timing is crucial to get anything you want.

An additional tactic I love in this space is: **"Decision Elasticity."** How much flawed data can I afford before it changes my decision?

It is easy to find a reason why your data is not perfect and even easier for companies to get stuck in discussing "which data is right".

You can argue that even data of a thermometer showing 5° can be wrong depending if it is lying in the sun or shadow. Yet even if it were 8°, your decision would be the same: Take your jacket.

Decision Elasticity is helping to conclude: "How much flawed data can our decision absorb and still be unchanged?" In other words, it would state that, "we would take this decision even if 18% of our data would be flawed or even random".

The way you calculate this is by simply adding an increasing amount of randomized data in your datasets and rerun your analysis until you reach the point of making a new decision. While p-value and R-Square are great significance measurements, Decision Elasticity can help you immensely in taking harder business decisions at a much higher confidence level.

If I had an hour to solve a problem, I would spend 55 minutes thinking about the problem and 5 minutes about the solution. - Albert Einstein

Micro-level machine learning

Micro-level machine learning is a group of algorithms that is based on their own data history. Forecasting the stock price of any company based on their historic numbers. Their past performance. Very effective for micro-behaviors, thus behaviors that are local/linked to only a company, a person, or a specific stock. You are basically exploiting human behaviors. Here is an experiment that you can do in almost every company. Go to your leadership team (8-15 people) and join 3 sessions. The content does not matter, but you will record where everyone is sitting, who is presenting, where is the screen and where is the door.

You will be able to build a prediction who will sit at which place in the fourth session.

As a result, you will see:
- That the presenters are usually at the front
- The smoker and those that are coming late that are in the back
- Those that slept together at the last Christmas party are close to each other but not too close
- Those that hate each other are on opposite isles
- That some are always next to their boss
- But also, that some people are never on the same spot (ironically their unpredictability makes them predictable)

Print out their names and stick them under the chairs of each member before the meeting starts.

Stand in front of the group, ask everyone to reach under their seat, and explain „that therefore AI and Data Analytics works. Humans are behavior driven. Routine gives us the illusion of control. Data represents the routines and that is what Data-driven decision-making tries to exploit. "

I am sure that you will be 90% correct. We are driven by our behaviors and are shaped by experiences.

Look at the below product sales:

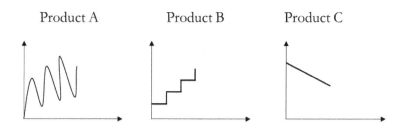

Based on the past data you can predict the future.

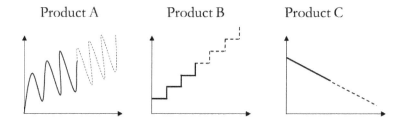

Marco-level machine learning

When you change the altitude on which machine learning is taking place you will reach macro-level machine learning. While micro-machine learning is great for learning based on its own data, so is macro learning the ability to learn from others and exploit the patterns others to predict your future or take other learnings from it.

What makes "macro-learning" so interesting is that it was largely a domain that enabled humans to become the predominant species on this planet. The ability to learn from others at an elevated magnitude is an amazing gift that we have now taught to machines.

Who of us needed to get hit by a car to learn that you better look left and right when crossing the street? You probably learned this from your parents. We learn from observing others and through following their teachings. When Netflix is recommending you what to watch next, they consider everyone else, extract their learnings, and then propose to you what to watch next.

They encapsulate many different types of algorithms and a sub-area is the over-pronounced yet underutilized "deep learning".

For example, based on the stock of competitors I can project other stock behaviors and a key aspect is that you can make predictions without having a great history about the item you are predicting yourself.

For example, based on products A, B, C above you can already judge product D even if it has only 3 data points.

Product D   Product D

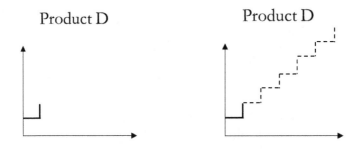

Applications of AI

You must consider that there are 3 main applications of AI from a company usage point.
1) exponential (augmented) decision making
2) new transformative (decision-based) business models
3) automated decision making or intelligent automation

The difference between them is along two dimensions. The number of times a problem needs to be solved/a decision needs to be taken and the impact the problem/decision has. If you have only a single decision (or few) but with high value, you are in exponential decision making.

If you have many decisions with a relatively low impact of each decision you are in the realm of automated decision making.

If it is a high impact decision on a highly recurring basis you are in the transformational/new business model space.

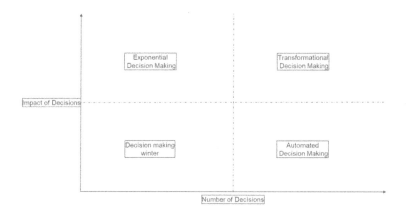

Let us take the example of a courthouse.

A courthouse like a business or in this case basically everything has millions of problems to solve and some of them can be answered by AI.

One typical issue is scheduling which case with which judge in which room should the judgment be held. To solve this, you could build a model that optimizes the coordination and learns for new data to adapt to specific issues.

This is an automated decision-making problem. You will need to take this decision multiple times per day but should you mess up and create a few delays this is unfortunate but not massively impactful.

In our courthouse example, we have the trial of the century ongoing, a presidential impeachment. Judges and jury are linked to the two-party system and are in a deadlock. You are being asked to build a model that interprets the law and looks at the evidence to provide an objective (as much as possible) judgment that will serve as the deciding vote. This is a very specialized exponentially (augmented) decision making problem with high stakes but the low probability that you will reuse the same model after this trial again, as every part of the AI is specialized in this case.

A new business model would be if we combine the impact of a decision and the high recurrence of the problem into completely replacing judges and have 80% cases judged by AI systems that evaluate law and evidence to provide fair and unbiased judgments. This is one step short of the movie minority report which includes the prediction component.

A typical mistake is that most companies start with a proof of concept on problems that are neither impactful nor numerous as they would like to reduce the risk of failure. Unfortunately, they end up in the "decision-making winter". Whatever you place here will not grow. If you would have used AI to build a facial recognition model that counts the number of people entering a single courtroom, you will have a specialized model that will have no impact and no reusability. It will stay forever a POC.

Novartis invested in Aktana, a company that provides AI-powered insights to sales reps to help them deliver the best relevant information to doctors, hospitals, and other caregivers. This Next-best action AI or smart analyst is a great example of automated augmented decision making. They give 100s of recommendations each day but the impact of each decision is relatively minimal.

xAi vs Deep Learning

In every AI or decision-making problem, you are constantly torn between two dimensions. On the one hand, you have the accuracy of every model that you build. On the other hand, you have the explainability of the model. In other words, can you explain to someone why the model has chosen why it did what it did? Insights have no value without action. It needs to lead to a decision to act.

Take the example of a cancer detection software. Would you rather have a model that is 98% accurate but the reasoning "why it assumes you have cancer" is too complicated for humans to understand or a model that is 90% accurate but everything is 100% explainable? Would you rather sit in a self-driving car that is better driving but you don't know why it would stop or accelerate at some points or in a car that is clear "why it does what it does" but is less accurate at it? Would you rather have a translation program that works better but does not explain to you why it translated each word as it did or rather a clear application explain why it did what it did even at lower accuracy of translation?

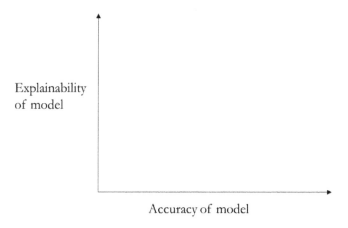

Well, while for the first two items it is rather controversial, the third case probably almost everyone is fine with the translation that works better. This links heavily to the dimension of impact we discussed before. The higher the impact of a decision the more we want transparency on why a decision has been taken. Imagine that you get a cancer drug prescribed, but the doctor has no information about why the AI said you need it. That does not make you feel good, right?

There are two variations of AI that focus on the extremes of these two dimensions, Deep learning & xAI(explainable AI).

Deep learning is a subset of AI. In most AI systems you have a similar flow on how to build an application.

- You collect data
- You split your data into training data and validation data (split data 80/20)
- You train your AI based on the training data
- You test your data on the validation dataset or test dataset
- If good, you use the model on a data set that you want to run the model or prediction on

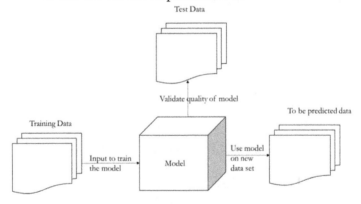

Take the example of credit card fraud. If we put next to each other "a normal development project" and "a normal AI Project" and "deep learning AI projects" where are the differences.

Normal Development	AI project e.g. with regression	Deep learning project
You collect historic data	You collect historic data	You collect historic data
You analyze existing data	You analyze existing data	You analyze existing data
You define which variables you need	You define which variables you need	**The Model** defines which variables you need
You define **rules** which impact variables have (e.g. you tell the model that an amount of 99.99 is increasing the probability of fraud)	**The Model** defines which impact variables have **individually** on the results (e.g. model defines based on past data that the euro amount x was a predictor for fraud)	**The Model** defines which impact variables have **individually** & **collectively** on the results (e.g. model defines based on past data that the euro amount is a predictor for fraud in a certain number of given cases if other conditions like the timing of invoice or date apply)
Test Results	Test Results	Test Results
Test Results & Run results on a live dataset	Test Results & Run results on a live dataset	Test Results & Run results on a live dataset

Basically, the key difference between AI and normal development is the actor who defines which impact individual variables have. E.g. for fraud detection **you** might build a rule that if the invoice is exactly 99.99 Euro it is a high chance of fraud based on your expert knowledge. Or that if you have more than 3 spelling mistakes it is a fraud.

In an AI with e.g. random forest or regression, **you** would give the model the variables like the number of spelling mistakes and amount and time of the day the invoice is received or who sent it. **The model** would select if it is 3 spelling mistakes or 2 or 4 or none are a predictor for fraud.

The more interesting difference comes from AI with random forest or regression and a deep learning AI. A "shallow" AI e.g. with regression has a few input variables, in this case, four input(time of invoice, amount, number of spelling mistakes, who sent the invoice) variables and two output variables(Fraud and No Fraud)

Input

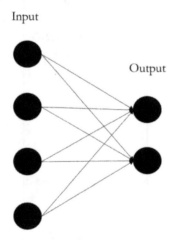

Output

It is an easy model where at the end it will tell that based on the past data if you will get an invoice in the future with 0 spelling mistakes but an amount of 99.99 Euro send from IBM is a fraud because in the model this amount and vendor were already caught as fake invoices. But most features are only seen in simple connections to each other.

In **deep learning** next to the input and output you have so-called hidden layers. These layers of neurons are combinations of multiple crossed inputs that create a complex algorithm in the backend and will identify cases we would not have even thought about. Hidden layers are usually not able to be read in-depth by normal reasoning which is why they are called hidden. This leads to high accuracy but low transparency on what has happened. Even if we could make it fully transparent does not mean we will really understand it, while it might be perfectly correct. Imagine the model would come out with the fact that an invoice is a fraud because it starts disproportionately often with the number 9. Benford's Law supports this model ideology, but we might not like this explanation.

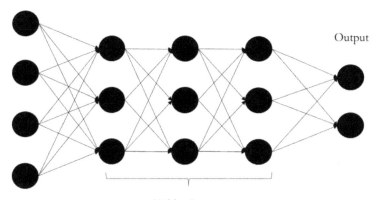

Input

Output

Hidden Layers

Unfortunately, not everything that is scientifically right makes sense does not need to make sense from a business perspective. The same goes for the other way. Or take: "I am 99% sure we should invest in a certain group of employees and it will generate a 15% increase in sales in 8.7 months, but I cannot tell you why."

Are you still able to use these results in a business context? Of course, but only if you consider some of the surrounding elements in addition to the actual analytics.

Allow me one personal observation, the analysts that were most successful in creating impact were not the ones that were the most mathematical knowledgeable but rather the most creative ones. Analytics is just as much creativity as it is analytical.

Explainable AI (XAI) is a technique that focuses on making machine learning reasoning understandable by humans. It is also known as interpretable AI or transparent machine learning. The idea of getting rid of the black box syndrome.
While the performance of deep neural networks has exceeded the human level in many complex tasks but to take action and to ensure people act according to the recommendation in many areas, we require transparency on why decisions have been taken.
Supporters of XAI say explainability will be the mediator between AI and society. It helps to build better models, remove bias, and will accelerate the next AI wave. Opponents of XAI say that we are basically dumbing down the machine to create arbitrary (often wrong) explanations so that we humans can understand what it says. Humans take most of the decisions unconsciously. We do not require an explanation in our own head but require it from an AI.

There are two approaches to XAI to choose from.
1) Build a transparent model from the start
2) Makes a black box algorithm more transparent afterward
Both are possible just requiring slightly different approaches.
It depends if you primarily focus on accuracy or primarily on explainability that you choose the approach.

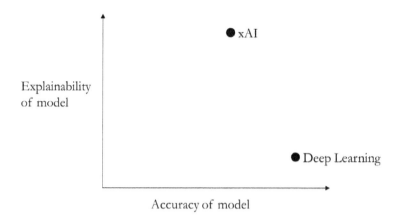

7 things you misunderstood about AI

When talking to friends, start-ups, and consultants seven misunderstandings came up quite often that caused issues in later discussion, valuations of start-ups, or project success.

Misunderstanding 1: 3 people talk about AI and mean 4 different things

If you come to a discussion around AI. Always split machine learning, from AI the product and "human-level" AI.

Misunderstanding 2: AI is new

The first AI system was written in 1951 by a guy called Christopher Strachey. It is far from new. Most algorithms of AI are 10-30 years old. What has changed is the computing power and creativity as well as the anchor in society.

Misunderstanding 3: Only because it says AI does not mean AI is in it

Be aware that when analyzing 30 different AI tools sold to businesses in only half of them any type of AI algorithm or ML algorithm has been used.

Misunderstanding 4: AI name

Siri, Alexa, Cortona. Why do people give AI systems a name? Have you named your laptop? Or your toaster? Interestingly AI systems with a name have a much higher acceptance rate than without.

Misunderstanding 5: You think you need Data lakes

AI systems can work on even small datasets. Micro-level machine learning algorithms like time-series work effectively even as of 25 data points.

Misunderstanding 6: There is an AI STANDARD

Today no two AI systems are the same. There are few till no standardization of AI modules. In your company do not yet invest in standardization until some clear winners have developed.

Misunderstanding 7: You invest not enough time on ethics

The further you move into augmented decision making the more you will need to think about ethics.

7 reasons why do you fail data science projects:

Unfortunately like every boom it contains a lot of shining and fake reality. In a recent survey to companies, 85% of data science projects either failed or delivered short of the expectations. Very few companies did see their bottom lines or balances sheets shift drastically. The following reasons were mentioned during the post-mortem.

Reason 1: You hired a Data scientist for a data science position Obviously, the area of data science is built around "Data scientists". The numbers magicians with a strong focus analytical skills and expertise on coding mostly in areas like R (open-source coding language, used at large scale in universities/companies because it's free) - phyton or other data science languages. In the past few years, the job received some god-fiction. And while the job is seen as a "new" type of job it actually exists for a very long time.

Unfortunately, there are multiple types of data scientists and you might want to be sure what you are hiring. You have 4 key new profiles in data science.

Core Pure Data scientists

Traditionally trained. Studied data science or mathematics or statistics. Ph.D. or equivalent. Have written multiple white papers. Long coding history. Often "area" agnostic, meaning they shift from a commercial project to and HR project to a medical project at ease. Often brought into projects to bring a "new point of view". The two main misunderstandings in projects are a leading failure in their projects
A) The academic bias often drives them into statistically relevant analysis but business irrelevant answers. They might provide a sales forecast of -1 trillion and are very happy about it. Why? Because the numbers hit the correct p-value and

because they were able to publish a whitepaper on how great their approach is.

B) Time is relative. If you come from an academic or research focus you apparently perceive goals and time differently. Many seasoned project managers pull their last hair in sprint reviews where no one finished a single user story or when everything is done "by the next week", for weeks every week.

You want **Core Pure Data scientists** in your projects when the mathematical value by far out ways the business relevance value especially in product design, science, medical research, etc.

Business Analytics Data scientists

These are business experts, finance experts, commercial analysts that learned to code and become very strong at it. They can combine business translation and coding/analytics in one person. High effectiveness due to the combination of what is needed and what is possible. But as every knowledge expert, they bring biases with them often reducing the "creative" side of things. As you feel you know your area well (both algorithms and business) you might just reproduce what you did in the past and learn less from others and new approaches. They often evolve out of existing positions like financial analysts or market research analysts or senior decision-makers. A key trend here is to make Data science a common skill like excel or PowerPoint.

You want **Business Analytics Data scientists** in your projects when the business relevance value by far out ways the mathematical value especially in company decision making, investment choices, top talent prediction, or intelligent automation.

A friend of mine liked to explain the difference with a controversial example: Does God exists?

A **pure data scientist** will look at calculating the probability that God exists based on all variables and then will say that

God does not exist with 65% probability. They try to create the objective truth.

A **business analytics data scientist** will look at the problem behind the problem. What is the so-what? Would you follow the gods' rules if he were existing? If you follow gods' rules and he does not exist, you lose nothing. If you do not follow gods' rules and he exists, you will suffer in the 7 circles of hell. Ergo it does not matter if he exists or not but to follow gods' rules creates higher chances of success. Input, probability & impact are well balanced to make sure you get as close as possible to the objective truth while ensuring the impact of everything is well understood.

Data science builders

Sometimes you do not just want to run a single analysis once. But you want to reproduce the results monthly with new data and gain new insights. Maybe with a user interface instead of a PowerPoint.
This brings whole new challenges as suddenly you must look more for sustainability, connectivity, security and access, distributed server models, effective cloud usage. Most pure data scientists hate this part, most business analysts do not know how to do it, thus a new cluster of data experts is evolved. Focused heavily on this niche often more build in python than in R or other "stronger" languages.

Analytics Business translator

Mostly finance or business experts that know enough analytics to use results and shape business questions into the right pieces needed for analytics while having significant business knowledge. They know their data and it's pitfalls and what future business events drive change. Seldom do they have coding experience or only limited but they do know how to apply analytics as adhoc or assets for which reason. They also translate each insight to concreate implementable actions.

Reason 2: Your project contains the letters POC or proof of concept

Proof of concepts have been born some time ago as a safe environment for failure when testing new technologies. Unfortunately, this has been over and misused so drastically that there is a strong negative correlation between the number of POC and success in technology implementations. The more POC the less success. Sounds counterintuitive? Not if you look at the starting point of a POC. The goal of the POC is to prove that a technology concept works, independent of the business question or the business impact. Thus, when it fails there is no harm. On the other side, the same goes for success. There are many POC that proofed that you could "use blockchain for working with suppliers".

Only once you want to use it with a real business question and on the scale, you will often find that other solutions might be more effective.

You can never start from technology and move to "what could it solve" but always from what are my problems and how can I solve them. You will need to open yourself to failure and accept that failure is part of real projects. You need to start with a real business problem that is great in ambition and be fully committed to solving it. During this project, you might need to test a few approaches/technologies, and some will fail but some will always work out. Be prepared to fail but don't separate the space for failure and impact of projects.

Reason 3: You staff your projects like you would staff other IT projects and look for people with experience

A colleague of mine draws me once a nice picture when he saw certain job postings in my department.

He rephrased:" innovative departments want to build the world first teleportation device in the world for long-distance traveling. Looking for a lead developer with 10 years in

teleportation, bringing new ideas, knows our internal processes especially all our abbreviations, has studied teleportation, preferable had their own company but want to work for others.
"

I have unfortunately seen too many data science projects staffed like an ERP rollout. With project manager that is looking for a blueprint in doing something that has often never been done. Staffed with an expert that talks about agile / design thinking but cannot connect it to the analytical approaches needed.

In analytics, you hire 1st for mindset, secondary for adaptability /learning speed, thirdly for behavior, and forth for skills.

Last year I took some time and went through all the CVs we received over the last 3 years and really spend time analyzing skills capabilities and the reason why I accepted them at the time.

Here are some curious things I found:
Most technology knowledge of specific technologies was outdated after less than a year. Many machine learning packages/tools used at a point in the past have completely abolished and replaced by TensorFlow from Google or others. Most reporting tool skills were completely disrupted - anyone with knowledge in SAP BW or Cognos BI quickly became irrelevant in the analytical space. Anyone who a few years ago had great knowledge in azure machine learning, lost largely their technology advantage when Microsoft decided to kill it and bring another tool themselves.
Technology experience is a useless decider for internal employees. Their knowledge could be outdated by the time they join your team. What is key is the ability to take the thinking of how to design solutions and migrate the thinking between different technologies.

Reason 4: You hire a large consulting company because you do not have a good internal team

Do not get me wrong. If you have the money and a good internal team, surround them with big consultancy companies. They could bring innovative approaches and fill the knowledge gaps that your team has - and be the fire accelerant on your wood foundation.

Yet if you do not have a strong team internal there will be a good chance that the project will not reach your goal, it will not be sustainable, and the cost will be exponentially more.

A few months after your projects have finished, one of your tech experts will analyze what has been done by the consultants to be able to replicate it or to learn from it. You will probably not enjoy the moment when he/she tells you that you paid 5 million dollars for something on the same level as high school math hidden under complicated slides and mathematical logic. No matter if you work on digitization, foundation, or digital transformation. Each time your internal teams are the key to sustainable success.

Data science projects are to a large extend cultural projects, no external company can be in your culture, your values, or your perspective.

Remember any project that you do should generate impact. Yet your engagement with the consulting company is only during the duration of the project long before impact is achieved.

Seems counterintuitive, right?

When you work with vendors you will need to ensure the incentives are linked to the goal of your project. The impact. While in the past especially with fixed-term contracts we forced the timing and budget constraints on the project, today you will need to put the constraints on value. KPI that rank from NPS or proven sales or proven cost reduction KPI.

Most vendors will not like this type of contract. The few that do should be your future long-term partners.

When working with external companies

A) always free up resources (to 100%) and mix them into the external company

B) Structure contracts with vendors differently into outcome-based contracts

---

Reason 5: You blame the data

Having data science projects is like having a car journey. And data problems are like traffic jams. If you do not prepare well, you get delayed or even temporarily stuck but you never are in real danger of not coming to your destination. A bad driver / or a bad destination is a much bigger problem. Your destination is your project goal, and nothing is worse than a bad destination.

Blaming the data is an excuse. There is always a way to get new data, better data, or calculate data at lower granularity. Even unclean data can provide great insights when you handle it well.

Even the absence of data is data.
During WWII the American air force was looking at all the bullet holes in their planes to identify which parts of their airplanes they need to strengthen. They looked where the planes most often got hit and which damage has been done. In the end, they saw that the fuel lines were much more often hit then the engine, so they started improving it. A great idea until soon after someone looked at the data and mentioned that the missing data is the key to the solution. The fact that we have data means that the airplanes managed to come back. Thus, they looked at the areas where they had no data about hits,

especially at the engines. Thus, creating data from missing data. Only then did they realize that they needed to strengthen the engines, not the rest. The absence of data is data in itself. Use it.

Reason 6: You aim too low

Get 10 students into a room. Split into two teams. Half you give a problem to look at your data and propose a way how you can save 5 million and one to save 50 million. Probably neither teams reached the goal, but the "50 million" team might propose an option to save 40 million whereas the other might even find the 5 million. But which result would you prefer? And is any of them a failure?

Our culture has fixed on the part of do not fly too high. But most people forgot that Daedalus warned Icarus not to fly too low. Aiming too low is as dangerous as aiming too high.

Reason 7: You have no clue what your problem is

Most projects in data science have an identity crisis. You do it because it seems everyone else is doing it, but you do not know your real problem. It is becoming part of the decision making winter. Either you just really wanted to do something in data science, or you have a too-small problem, or you ask the wrong questions. Often, we know what we want to get out but are not able to ask the right questions.

How to get better at decision-making projects

Product development in analytics is the art of transforming a problem into a solution that can be temporary as an ad-hoc analysis or long term reproducible real assets.

When I hire Data Scientists for internal positions or projects, I always ask a question: what the most difficult part of an analytics project is. The biggest difficulty is the business question/problem.

The business question is encapsulating the impact you want to achieve from it, give guidance on what should be a result, and drives the value you are hoping to generate.

One problem comes from the right sizing.
A question should not be too big as otherwise your project does not know where to start and where to end.
For example, do not start a project on: "How to triple our sales."
It will end in a mess.

On the other side, a too-small business question does add too much bias and does not leave room to look for alternatives.
"Which of our two advertisement channels (tv or radio) should I invest to triple our sales by acquiring more female customers".

The problem with this question is that:
A) It implies the bias that sales are dependent on this advertising heavily, while it could be possible the ads do not have any sales impact and it is purely based on the mouth to mouth marketing or sales reps.
B) It implies an either-or solution while a mix could be more reasonable
C) It adds the assumption that women are to be targeted. If this is based on facts supporting the strategy than good but most likely you do not know if women are the right target group for these advertisements.

(Tactic) Business question rephrasing techniques

Most business questions you want to answer need to be reframed to reach the question behind the question. Here are a couple of key techniques you can use to check and challenge your business question relevance.

Remember each business question you cover needs to be focused on the right timing, needs to be actionable, and focused on the right audience. For that in the first technique, we are going to reframe an example question according to 5 key dimensions.
Let us take a business question that many companies have as an example:

„What has been our most effective marketing investments of the past?"

It sounds like a good question, but it has a few challenges embedded in it. To identify if the question is really the best question we want to answer and if there is a question behind the question, we are going to shift the question along each of the axes.
The first axis is time. If we were to shift the question focusing on past, present, and future how would the question look like?

Past	Present	Future

- Past version: What have been our most effective marketing investment of the past
- Present version: What are the most effective marketing investments currently
- Future version: What will be the most effective marketing investments

The subtle difference in question is significantly changing the direction of the analysis you will need to execute. If your focus on the past version of the question your key focus will be on analyzing your past performance, how you invested and what your returns were, yet you might miss considering if the past ecosystem and future ecosystem are still in alignment. Too often in projects, a great analysis was later invalidated by not considering a change in the environment.

If you look at the present version of the question you look at really the latest investments but also at what the competition is doing today.

If you look at the future version of the question you will focus also on how the ecosystem is evolving as well as on what are the best investment trends to do a prediction on where to best invest.

Next, we will shift the questions according to actionability. Meaning are we able to do anything with the answer? This is a key point in the exercise as any nonactionable question needs to be disregarded.

Next, we shift the question according to the actor frame. The actor frame is to reframe the point of view according to each actor involved and see which question we are most interested in.

- What will be the most effective marketing investments in our competition?
- Which marketing investment will make our company a market leader?
- What will be the most effective investments of our marketing staff?
- What will be the most effective marketing investments in the eyes of our customers?
- What will be the most effective marketing investments in the market?
- What will be the most effective marketing investments for the families of our customers?
- What will be the most effective marketing investments where we can collaborate with our partners and vendors?

In this case, we will choose "What will be the most effective marketing investments of the eyes of our customers." The key difference from the original question is that we are now looking at improving our sales and not reducing our costs.

Next, we will shift the question between a general frame, and specialized frames. These frames could be geographical. Do we analyze each country together or a few countries or a single country?
The frame can also be specialized in specific marketing channels or overall market channels.

In this case, we are choosing "What will be the most effective marketing investments of eyes of our customers in Europe within the next 3 years across all our marketing channels" (to avoid a biased question).

The second technique is the **reversal technique**, which is used by simply reversing in the example question 1 or 2 words.
Transition "What are the most effective marketing channels in the future" towards "What are the least effective marketing channels in the future." This is helpful to see alternative approaches to solving the same problem.

The third technique is **the 5 whys**? Asking the person who raised the question 5 times why to figure out what the real question in his/her thoughts was.

The fourth technique and my preferred is the **Nostradamus session** (see change management tactics chapter).

Algorithms you need to know

In the next part, we are going to look at a few algorithms that are typically used in augmented decision making and how they reflect the two previous dimensions of explainability and accuracy.
For that, we are going to look at the simple example of the likelihood of shooting goals in soccer of a given player.

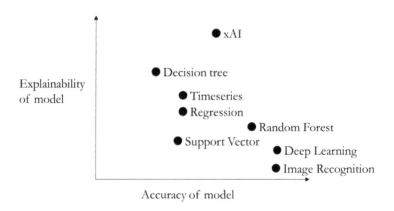

Regression & Correlation

Correlation describes the statistical connection/relationship between 2 variables. In other words, how are the two variables connected to each other? The results are usually on a scale of -1 to 1. One(1) meaning the higher the one the higher the other. -1 meaning the lower one the higher the other. 0 meaning the two variables are independent of each other.

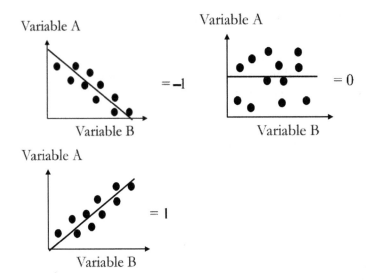

In the example of soccer if we look at the distance to the goal and the % of goals shot.

We will ask a soccer player to start near the goal and each time starts shooting a few times on the goal. Afterward, the player will move back 5 meters. We will measure how much % of the goals the player shot each time.

- At 0 meter distance, the player shot 100% goals
- At 10 meters distance, the player shot 90% goals
- At 20 meters distance, the player shot 80% goals
- At 50 meters distance, the player shot 50% goals
- At 100 meters distance, the player shot 0% goals

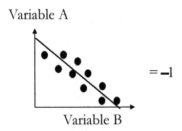

The result in the correlation is close to -1. Meaning the further you are from the goal the less likely you are scoring. But the number does not give you how exactly the two are linked. To measure this, we are trying to use regression.

Regression is a statistical method used that determines the **strength and direction** of the relationship between one dependent variable and a series of other variables. These can be a single variable or multiple.

In the example above, we would use regression to receive the following formula as a result.

$$\% \, Goals \, = 100 + (Distance * -1\,)$$

E.g. % Goals at a distance of 40 would be 60 = (100 – 40).

This is a univariable linear regression. Now, we do not need data science to reach this conclusion. But it gets more interesting if we add one or multiple additional variables.

Goalkeeper	Distance	Goal %
0	0	100
0	10	90
0	20	80
0	50	50
0	100	0
1	0	50
1	10	45
1	20	40
1	50	20
1	100	0

$$\% \, Goals \, = 91 + (Distance * -0.75\,) + (Goalkeeper * -33)$$

This is a multivariable linear regression. This can include a large array of variables and can if results are significant give a great indication of what variable has which impact.

In most cases in business, you will not have a linear but non-linear regression. Meaning you will have curves instead of straight lines. E.g. you have the rules of distinguishing return. As of one-point investments will not have the same impact they had initially.

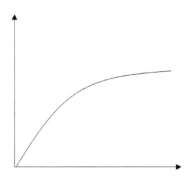

KNN

Basically, what KNN does is what most businesses try to do for years: Benchmarking. Or better KNN is finding the closest nearest neighbor (s). K standing for the number of closest neighbors. Sometimes this technique is also called digital twin, but this wording has been taken over in a different digital twin model that looks at digital "twins" of physical actors or objects. You are basically looking at e.g. multiple companies with multiple variables (headcount, revenue, growth), etc. And find in a database the 1 or more digital twins/nearest neighbors. Depending on the input parameters you provide you can find the closest matches within the same industry or across on a normalized dimension.
You can take the assumption of one company or the other.

Examples:

In one company this was used to find for employees which type of training is more likely to work. Thus, looking at for new employees looking for their nearest neighbor and the based on the neighbor feedback about existing training to judge if that might be a good fit (some people prefer F2f training, some online, etc).

Going back to our example it would be looking at a new player that we have 0 historic information about. He/she has never shot on the goal. So we are going to take other players that are most similar to that person according to what we know e.g. height, stronger foot, age, gender, etc). Based on whoever is closest to our player (and their history of goal scoring) we will predict the probability to shoot the goal.

Decision tree

Everyone who went to business school and most during their time at school has seen decision trees. A tree starting from the root splitting in more and more arms each time with an „if-then-else "or „ conditional split."

Take the example of "what training should you provide to employee x" using the parameters of level in organization and time in the position. Using this you will build the following tree

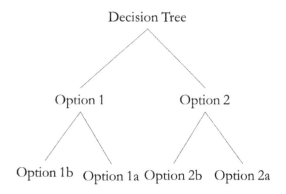

In this case, you will create a tree that says if the employee is in the company for less than 5 years and is in a management position, he will prefer a leadership training F2F.

In our soccer example it might be:
- Is the distance below 30 meters?
  - If yes, Is there a goalkeeper
    - Yes, then there is a 50% chance
    - No, then there is an 80% chance
  - If no, Is there a goalkeeper
    - Yes, then there is a 10% chance
    - No, then there is a 40% chance

Random forest

A random forest is basically multiple decision trees where the parameters get randomly selected.
Multiple TREE = FOREST
Random parameter selection = random
= Random Forest

Aside from the creative name selection, it is an extremely powerful algorithm for prediction in a business environment.

Imagine the previous case only that you will have 15 attributes and you do not know which of these attributes are impacting the problem. The idea is to build as many trees and we are going to randomly select a few of the attributes for each of these trees. After building a few thousand trees we are going to look at
1) which variables are the most impactful
2) taken a simple majority of the decision problems. You take the result that more than 50% of trees have recommended.

Only when you present the results do not talk about the fact that you used a random forest. Any presentation that contains random decision making will give a lot less buy-in. Shift the discussion towards the fact that you are building a large number of decision trees as it connects to their "management history".

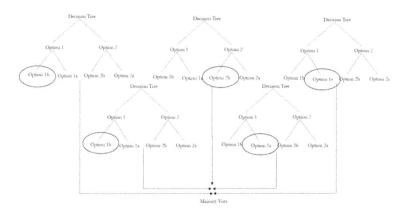

Take the example of our soccer case. Imagine you have 10 variables like distance to the goal if there is a goalkeeper, how long the player is playing, what their primary position is, how much air is in the ball, how wet the ground is, etc.

The random forest would build a larger number of trees like in the decision tree example before only it would each time select a few out of the 10 variables randomly.

In one tree it might select the distance and if there is a goalkeeper. In another, it might select how wet the ground is and the distance to the goal. And so on.

In the end, each tree will be evaluated e.g. 30 trees. And the prediction, if the player will shoot a goal, will depend on what most trees are saying.

Timeseries

Timeseries like Arima, STL, or ETS are usually considered forecasting models. You use them specially to identify trends, seasonality, and outliers.

You could use it on the stock market by for example looking at data of the last 48 months.

Timeseries models usually then split this into

   a) Trend

   b) Seasonality

   c) Outliers

Imagine sales of flowers at a small shop. No matter what you do with your investments you will always have a seasonality impact in which on holidays you will sell more than on nonholidays and during winter your average sales will drop even if you are in an upward trend.

In our soccer example, it might be that we see the trend that players at the beginning of the game have a higher chance of succeeding than after 80 minutes due to exhaustion. In this case, we might see that a certain player is on an upward trend that game after game the player is having a better probability of shooting a goal but in terms of seasonality he will perform worse at the end of each game.

Timeseries and regression can be combined to use multiple variables in addition to time, trend, and seasonality.

The last concept in this context is lag. Some variables have a direct impact, some will take time until they have an impact. Most of your investments will not lead to a direct sales increase in the same month but only a few months later.

In our soccer case, it might be that it starts raining but the impact of the rain (wet ground) will take time to materialize.

Text analytics

Text analytics in most cases is part of broader classification algorithms.

Classifications consist of two stages: the learning stage and the prediction stage. The learning stage entails training the classification model by running a designated set of past data. The goal is to teach your model what to extract and then use these learnings on new sets of data.

Text analytics problems are categorized into infinite classification and finite classification.
A finite classification means you have a potentially large but countable number of potential data to be classified.
On the other hand, your infinite data classification which means that the number of potential words that could fall in each category are endless.
Imagine trying to find out how many company names have been mentioned in the last 100 published business books (infinite data / infinite company names), versus how often in these books is google, apple or Microsoft mentioned(finite).

This includes natural language understanding, text summarization, natural language generation, and natural language processing as well as sentiment, perception analytics, and translation.

In our soccer example, we could read the written reports of each of our scouts to predict based on their written input which player will most likely be the best goal scorer.

Timeline analytics

Timeline analytics is part of storytelling algorithms rather than traditional data science. It is using a multivariable dataset over a larger time period to explain what has happened at key steps.

Step 1: Draw a timelines graph of your variable you want to explain e.g. Sales.
Step 2: Identify breakpoints, valleys, and hills.
Step 3: Identify which variables have changed shortly before or after the breakpoints to explain them. Did the price change? Did we invest in something else?

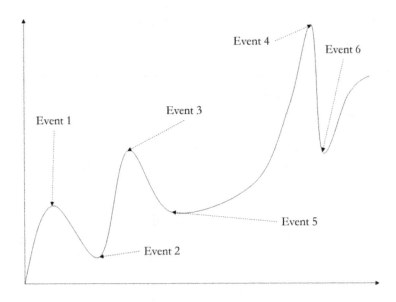

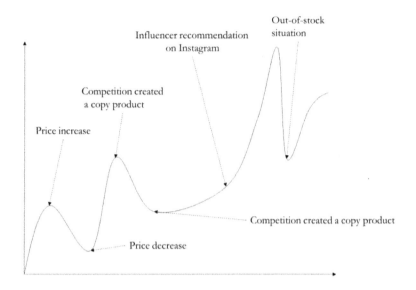

Reinforcement Learning

Next to the random forest, this is my favorite area of algorithms. Largely because it is how even a dog is trained.

Reinforcement learning is basically consisting of an environment, one or multiple actors, and reward.
The goal is that the actor by itself given a few possible actions can learn the best path forward.
How does it work?

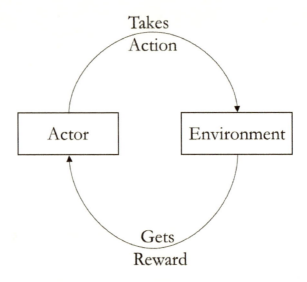

Basically, you define an actor e.g. Super Mario. Super Mario is an old side-scrolling classic. In this case, the goal is that super Mario gets from the left side of the screen to the right side of the screen without being hit by his enemy that is running his way. To do this he can walk left, right, stand, or jump. What reinforcement learning does is that you define a reward function. In this case, the faster super Mario gets from left to right without being killed. The faster, the higher the reward function (a counter basically). If he gets hit, he loses points. Every second the reward counter goes down. If he is getting closer to the goal the reward goes up.

What will now happen is that Super Mario, who has no clue what it means to jump, or walk will choose to take an action. E.g. walk right. He will have an input on if there are enemies around him and if there is a hole in the ground.
The first few tries Mario will run to the right (reward function going up) and fall into a hole(reward going down). The next time he reaches the hole he will try a different action like going left or maybe jumping. He will try things till he finds an action

given the input of the environment (there is a hole in front of you) that gives results (reward function up) than other actions. Over time Mario will play millions of games but at the end be the best super Mario player the world has ever seen.

This is extremely powerful to build environments for testing, medical research, game theory, decision making, and others.

As I said, this is how we train dogs. You say the command "Sit". You wait till he sits and gives your dog a treat(reward). If he does not understand or does something else he does not get the treat. After a few tries, he will understand that "Sit" means "all paws and butt on the ground" and he will do it.

It will be a major milestone in robotics, self-driving cars, and business decision making.

7 biggest mistakes you do when making decisions without data

1) Anchor bias

The average life expectancy in India in 1947 was 31 years. How old was Gandhi when he was assassinated?

Gandhi died at an age of 78 years. Yet the curious thing is that based on the first fact that only is very loosely connected to Gandhi you probably guessed a much lower number than if I would have given you another fact like the life expectancy in India of politicians is 3x as high as normal citizens.

We run this as a couple of experiments in 2 groups of 20. We gave them exactly the two questions you saw above.

When evaluated the results we saw that the first group's prediction was 53 vs 72 of the second group. This is called an anchor bias.

It is a bias where you are given an initial piece of information way too much relevance in the following discussion. It is often used in price negotiations or other sales pitches where we get way too much influenced by the first info we get.

2) Historic bias

History is written by the victors. Yet we assume that only because someone else has experienced the past and recall it in their own way. In your companies, you will often listen to how things worked by those that were part of the company during the last reorganization or during the last project. Only because someone was there does not mean the will give an accurate account of what really happened.

3) Optimism/ pessimism bias

This is a bias where either you always believe bad things never will happen to you or where you believe they always happen to you. Either way, they drive you towards an unnecessary low or high-risk appetite.

4) Cover your ass bias

We like to look better than we are. We try to imagine or connect information so selective that we do not look bad. You and your team members will often adjust information in a way that protects you even if it leaves out pieces of information about the objective truth.

5) Dunning Kruger Effect

The tendency for unskilled individuals/organizations to overestimate their own abilities and for experts to underestimate their own abilities.

It's ironic how this can affect whole companies when you see companies that are great at example launching products will only see problems in their way but companies that never did any digital ventures how they believe they are better than the competition.

6) You have enough data facts that could prove you wrong

One of our main reasons why we do not like data is simply that it can prove we are wrong. We hate to be wrong. And worse is if someone can prove we are wrong. One way is to avoid using data in decision making. The better approach is that we need to start thinking more that we are always wrong and using data will help us to get less wrong.

7) Eyewitness bias

We all believe that we are right, and we like to believe others on what they saw. "I only believe it if I see it!". You all know the saying. Is it not ironic that eyewitness testimony is so much seen as credible yet if someone says they saw a UFO we would not take it as proof that extraterrestrial life exists? Eyewitness is in science the least trustworthy source of information and even in business, we should consider it always with a grain of salt. Despite that in the court of law eyewitnesses are the most believable evidence that there is.

7 biggest mistakes you do when making decisions only based on data

1) Do not confuse statistically correct answers with business-relevant answers

This is an experience that many data scientists and academics have when entering their business world. In analytics we have answers where the R square (indicator for significance) is great or the p-value (another indicator for significance) is below 0.05 or the results are significant but from a business side, it is completely irrelevant. It is, unfortunately, true, but I have yet to see a project convincing their customers or even their management that their recommendation is the right one because of statistical figures like R2 or correlation numbers alone. You have obvious cases that most of us know from childhood e.g. the correlation between the number of cancer cases in the world and the number of garbage trucks in the world. They have a strong significant positive relation from the numbers side but logically untrue. You cannot sell more medicine for cancer than there are cancer patients, no matter how good your R2 is. It might sometimes lead to better results if you take a number that is not statistically relevant but surround it with business acumen so that you can trigger the needed discussions.

---

*Always balance your data with Business
knowledge and include market patterns into your
data to improve*

---

2) Even facts need interpretations

It is a fact that we have 110 sales reps. It is a fact that our sales increased by 10% when we increase sales reps from 100 to 110. It is a fact that we have a strong positive correlation. Putting these things together and consider outside effects or hidden connection variables that we might not have included - to finally turn them into a real story will be required to make anything we do business relevant.

---

*Numbers need interpretation & need to be
brought into a consistent story that includes the
right context information*

---

3) Analysis paralysis

When running analysis, you can easily reach a stage of analysis paralysis where you continuously keep analyzing facts before acting on them. It is the business version of gambling addiction. You want to be more and more sure of what you are seeing. You try to reach a 100% information basis but this will never work and if you miss the fact that each day that you do not present your analysis you are simply supporting the status quo.

4) Your Data is biased, just different types of biases than humans

Data helps us get rid of human biases, which does not mean that it does not have a bias on its own. Most datasets are human-generated or human-derived.

This was seen in many examples not least in a case that Google shared some time ago. The first case was around recruitment via AI. Analyzing CVs of candidates and predicting which will be the best talents for the company. It looked at the history of top talents within the company and compared it to the features of the new applicants. Normally a great use case for the power of AI.

It failed on one premise, which was that the past hires were well selected and top talents were unbiased selected. This was not the case. Humans did the recruitment and did the selection of top talents. The result was biased data on which the AI learned which caused the system to discriminate against women on a large scale.

5) If your analysis is created by a developer it has biases

A secondary part of bias is often forgotten. AI Systems are learning by itself, but they all got build by a human (so far). Any rules or constraints that the developer was considering relevant will influence any decisions long ago.

In a couple of years, you will probably realize that some AI recommendations are based on the biased constraints of a developer that has left the company long ago.

For any critical software have another project independent analyst review code & analysis for bias

---

6) You never have enough data

You never have as much data as you would like to have. You can always create data, even if it might take some time. More data is not always better. There is always something you can do with the data you have.

Deal with the cards you are given

---

7) You can run 20 algorithms on the same data and could get 20 outputs and all of them are correct in itself

I love and hate this aspect of analytics. Each algorithm from Arima (Autoregressive-Moving Average) to STL (Seasonal Trend decomposition using Loess) to random forests to deep learning they all have been built by humans and have their own strength weakness as well as constraints.
You might want to do a forecast using the data you have, you run all algorithms and you get 5 different numbers. Which of them is right? All of them, but all in a different setting considering different assumptions. It might be how they considered outliers, it might be that they considered corona to be a one-time event or a yearly event.

Always derive the assumptions from your model in a business language to discuss if they are providing the right guidance.

(Tactic) Digital Technology Capitalisation

In this chapter, we are going to look at the different technologies that are being considered part of the digital world and are at your disposal for your business. At one point or the other, you will come into contact with them and this section should help you navigate the bluffs that technology vendors throw your way, key lessons about when to use them, and when they fail as well as to inspire your thinking about each of them. In a book I read lately technologies were clustered in various ways including into "transformative technologies" and "enabling technologies" and while this concept is bringing some interesting perspective on the potential of different technologies it is missing the key point of technologies - ALL technologies are enablers and technology in itself is never transformative. Only HOW you use the technologies can be transformative. A blockchain is worth nothing if it is not used. A car engine is not transforming how transportation but how it is used as a part of a car and part of a bigger ecosystem including fuel stations and traffic rules.

This confusion of separation of technologies and business models/technology applications led me to introduce a different perspective by looking at commonly named "technologies" and split them into three groups:

- Application/Business Models of technologies
- Technology groups
- Technologies

The first group is about how one or multiple technologies were put into an orchestrated product, business model, or ecosystem. Artificial intelligence is the application of multiple different ML approaches combined with UX or process embedding technologies. HTML is the technology, websites the technology group, and a webshop a specific business model combined with technology application.

Most technologies are actually not singular technologies but groups. There are many different ML algorithms under the umbrella of machine learning. Technologies are the core technical foundations of the digital world. They include programming languages, network protocols, and hardware components.

E.g. HTML (the programming language & protocol) is a technology.

None of the technologies are new; nothing prevented us from creating all the things 10 - 20 years ago.
It is a creative journey, a solution journey, a transformation journey. It is a journey that is lost or won in the mind of people, not on their laptops.
But to understand the rules of the game and the cards you are given let us look at a few key technologies, groups, and business models.

Aspects of RPA - robotics process automation

In recent years RPA tools have been reaching a hype mode and leverage from a large interest in AI and robotics in the market. Now let us be clear RPA is not AI and RPA is probably not even what most senior managers expect from a robot. RPA is a patchwork and RPA is a macro. How does RPA work? RPA basically records individual steps in a process and repeats them 1 to 1. For example, you open an excel file, you copy two values into SAP, you copy two more value to another platform and copy the results of all into an email and send it. The RPA would save this action and would be able to repeat this step by step with potentially a few dynamic entry paraments (e.g. entering different data). If you would click 2x left and 1x right it would repeat the same. If you would have closed one window by error, the RPA would every time it runs close and open the window.

The example above shows you the main strength of RPA cross-system automation. For a case like above, most companies would need at least 4 different IT developers and probably 8 managers on top of that to code a real interface that would be fully automated. On the other side, you should never use RPA to automate within a single system as the downside is the patchwork mode. You replicate what humans do. Not improve it. You keep the same error risks and are limited by the performance of the screens and the tool. Rather than improving the process and using the systems to its maximum. Also, should any visual items of your screen change most robots will fail and you need to record every process variation from scratch?

Why then do especially finance, hr, and business departments run towards RPA?

The profound reason is that RPA allows automation without IT and has short/mid-term the same value generation at lower cost & effort. Most departments hate being dependent on IT departments. Not understanding their process, consider their processes outdated and useless, and that the IT experts are less well placed in driving effective automation. Is it true? Maybe? Creating a robot to run some transactions is 80% business/process knowledge and 20% technical while normal automation was the exact opposite. As a counter, IT teams are pushing for RPA COE(center of excellence) or factories which is a logical way of looking at control of power but does not reflect the nature of the technology and is built on the logic of past technology ideologies. It does not mean any governance it means simply don't centralize if the knowledge that is needed is decentralized by nature. Don't buy RPA just to avoid your IT department - fix the collaboration.

RPA is an enabling technology that accelerates processes but has very few transformational opportunities.

There is often talk of OCR. OCR as optical character recognition is a quite old technology that has improved drastically over time and is embedded in my different RPA systems. It is used to read e.g. PDF or paper scans and identify characters on the paper to make it machine-readable. Often used in financial applications in areas like invoice management to easily scan an invoice and copy all relevant information into the required systems input fields without manual input. Most RPA system OCR capabilities are quite well advanced if you are in the English-speaking environment or in the Latin alphabet.

The area of intelligent RPA is in 2020 still very early and while every RPA software promises intelligence, thus AI-supported automation, very few use any AI technology.

The next time an RPA software seller talks about their AI capability please ask him or her what technology is being used. Behind most "intelligent RPA" is an "If then else statement" coded by a human.

Does that mean that RPA is not worth the investment? Absolutely not. It has a place in any midsize or largescale company. But it is not the solution to all your problems. First, identify which problems you want to solve and then see if RPA is the right solution for it.

7 Changes drones & true robotics will bring

Compared to RPA, true robotics is about optimizing physical processes or automating physical movements. Think about the 100% automated warehouses. Think about the 100% automated factories. Think autonomous trucks. Think of drone delivery.

Today there is a wave of outsourcing that gets brought back to Europe simply because building a 100% automated factory is cheaper than outsourcing to a low-income country. Robotics is also evolving at a much higher speed than what you are perceiving. Look at Boston dynamic robots between 2009 and 2019.

- 2009 – can walk slowly on even ground, Heel to toe human walking, 3.2 mph

- 2011 – Ability to move arms, ability to kneel, ability to do push-ups
- 2013 – walking on uneven ground, standing on one leg
- 2016 – Ability to get up after being pushed down, ability to pick up things, open doors, walk outside
- 2017 - Ability to jump between different heights, Ability to do a backflip
- 2018 - Ability to run, parkour level jumps
- 2019 - Gymnastics including handstand, turns, rolls, etc

What are some of the impacts we will see?

1) They will reduce drastically manual work
   Physical work will change drastically. Drones & true robotics will boom in the mid-20s. Lower class and mid-class jobs will be drastically changed
2) They will change the way wars are being fought
   Drones will make up the majority of army fights as of 2028
3) They will change police and emergency work
   Drones are already employed by multiple police agencies. Especially during times of racial discrimination by police, unbiased robotics will get a boost.
4) They will change the way we send packages
   You will get packages delivered to you in before 2030 by a drone or robot.
5) Your children will grow up in a work where robots and drones are part of daily life
   The new generation will learn to live with robots on daily basis.
6) We work on functions but not ethics
   Today the most effort is spent on improving the functionalities of robotics. Walking. Jumping. Lifting.

In the next 10 years, the focus will be on the right level of ethics and limited bias.

7) Social media addict to robot addict
After a social media addiction, there will be a robotic addiction to improve our daily life resulting in a partially lazier society.

7 Misconceptions of Chatbots (Technology application)

1) Chatbots are not a technology

A chatbot is not a technology group in itself but an application of either AI or rule-based systems connected to a messenger app like a Facebook messenger or WhatsApp or a separate website. The idea to provide 24/7 support to customers while reducing the cost of call centers has caused a misinterpreted boom in this perceived "technology".

2) Most chatbots do not contain any AI elements

9 out of 10 chatbots are not AI enabled in any sense. They are "if then else" statements. Like a decision tree that allows x amount of questions and has x amount of answer prepared.

3) NLP, NLU, NPG?

Natural language processing, Natural language understanding, and Natural language generation are three core aspects of intelligent AI systems.

In most chatbots, the process of answering questions goes the following

a) A text is being analyzed and a ranking along different **intents** is being calculated. Intent meaning a distinct group of questions. For example, you might have in your chatbot two intents. The first covering "Ordering" (I want to order this dog food) question and the second "delivery" type of questions (Where is my delivery). Thus, each sentence in the chatbot will evaluate if what the users have asked linked to intent 1 or intent 2.

b) **Entity** recognition will follow. Each word will be analyzed if it fits in a category of words. In our dog food example, this means that a sentence like:

"I would like to order 15 cans of Superdogfood" will be split and each word will be categorized, and filler words like "of" will be removed.

- I= Person
- order = action
- 15 cans = Amount
- "Superdogfood" = Product

c) An **answer** for a given intent and given entities will be given. Should one required entity be missing then it might ask additional information like: "For when would you like the product"
or if all entities required are provided it will use a template answer like:
"Thank you! I would like to confirm that you want [Amount] of [Product] for [Date] delivered to your home at [Address]."

4) Chatbot as the first line of defense, not the last
Most chatbots that are effective have meanwhile established themselves as the first line of getting questions. Only if answers cannot be answered by the chatbot it will go towards the human-powered helpdesk.

5) Chatbot humor and personality
Another successful trip was the fact that chatbots with a sense of humor are creating a better experience than pure fact-based

chatbots. Just like in humans a personality will make a difference.

6) Name your Chatbot

Chatbots without names are getting a 30% lower positive feedback score.

7) Not everyone wants to talk to chatbots
Always look at your complete customer base. There is a good chance not all customers are willing to reach out to a chatbot.

7 aspects to evaluate for self-service reporting (technology group)

1) Everyone hates reporting, and everyone loves reporting
Reporting jobs are never seen in a company as exciting jobs. No matter if it is financial reporting, HR reports, or sales reports. In most cases, people creating the reports are last on the recognition list and first on the blame lists. Everyone hates reporting but without reporting, we are flying blind. Management looks at reports every day. Most companies have standard reports that are created on a monthly or daily basis.

2) Reporting and analytics are not the same
Reports are not analytics or even insights. Reporting requires the reader to interpret the number and contextualize themself. Comments and visualization are supposed to help.

3) Do not use best practices of 20 years ago on technologies of the last 3
Reporting tools have changed. We need to adopt our best practice.

4) Self-service reporting can be your heaven or your hell depending on culture/skills and capability

Self-service reporting, in other words, the ability to create reports as individual users and not as a centralized team e.g. IT has been a major promise but often ended in disaster. Many blame technologies. But the issue often comes from a missing culture and governance. Doing things in self-services requires twice the governance a normal report requires. Ensuring access, data privacy, data quality, and the right definitions are complicated.

5) Qlik vs Tableau
Reporting technologies like Qlik and Tableau are key leaders in the Bi / Reporting platforms.

Who uses Tableau: Wells Fargo, Apple, Capital One, US bank
Who uses Qlik sense: Accenture, Canon, Deloitte, BMW, Fila

6) Key Features
What are the features used to evaluate today's reporting platforms?
- Ease of use
- Advanced analytics
- Data Modelling
- Cost factor
- Operating support
- Reference clients
- Security

7) Invest in information systems not reporting systems
One thing that you want to consider is that you rather want an insight system or information system rather than a pure reporting system. Due to the rise of contextualized data and insights, it will be more important to store the insights rather than just the raw data used to derive the insights.

7 aspects of the Platform business (technology application)

In 2019 the top ten best-performing companies(financially) in the world were Apple, Microsoft, Amazon, Google (Alphabet), Berkshire Hathaway, Facebook. Alibaba, Tencent, JP Morgan Chase, and Johnson & Johnson.
What do 7 of these 10 have in common? They are platform businesses (to at least 20% of revenue come from platforms).

Aspect 1: A platform is as much as a business model as it is a technology utilization. A platform in simple terms is a marketplace. This means they organize content/services/products, make it available, and easily accessible. Their goal is to create value by aggregating fragmented markets and to connect consumers with either other consumers, with content creators, or with service providers while having no or limited assets themself.
UberEATS does not own any of the restaurants. Uber does not own any cars. Booking.com does not own hotels. Airbnb does not own apartments. Apple does not own the music nor the majority of apps.
You create a place where others can sell their services, create, and share content, offer advice, raise questions, and create communities. You create a more closely connected world.
Platforms allow users to have a single place to find holistic access to many different opportunities while suppliers of services or products get direct access to many customers with limited or only directed marketing.
Every one of us is using Amazon or Alibaba to make purchases. And the experience of a single place to get all your items with an ease of single payment and single delivery is making your life easier.
Imagine the difference in the experience of buying 10 products either on amazon or via 10 different supplier websites each time with a new registration, ten times entering your address as well as credit card payments.

The concept is not new. A non-digital version of this is the example of Walmart and the shopping center. Rather than going to 10 shops you just went to Walmart or a shopping center like the German KaDeWe or the London Harrods or the New York Macys.

Aspect 2: Does this mean that platform business is always superior to individual websites?
To answer this let us look at the examples from the non-digital world. Take the Apple stores. Why would you go to an Apple store if they could get all the devices at an electronic store but also allow you to view all competition products and maybe buy some other needed products?
The key here is experience and unique value proposition in terms of e.g. services. The physical shops that today are striving are remarkable at either delivering an experience that you cannot find in big stores or better surrounding services which outperform the value loss of not being part of the "cross-brand retailer".

Aspect 3: Platform business models come in different variations
a) Advertisement based: This means your platform is most likely free to log in and you make most of your money with advertisement. Having users see an advertisement and clicking on it will give you 0.5$ to 5$ if you use services like Google AdSense. Their big advantage is that they adapt the advertisement to your website content thus avoiding that on your platform for healthcare you show ads for car engine parts. Alternatively, you rent ad space. You usually calculate the CPM as e.g. 5$. The CPM is the cost per mile (translated into "cost per thousand") meaning that you get (5$) as monthly income for 1000 users of your platform (if it has a front end). If you get 1m visitors on your website per month, then this would generate a paycheck of 500$ per month for each banner of your

main page. There are multiple website services you can use for this like BuySellAds.

b) Freemium or Premium:
This basically means platform customers need to pay to join your platform. This can be one-sided meaning only "service providers" are paying on your platform but customers not, or it can be all parties need to pay to join.

c) Commission based:
This is an obvious model if on your platform products or services will be sold. In this case, you will take a commission of x% of the overall product or service price. For example, Amazon is taking 15% of the overall selling price of any product that someone sells on its platform.

d) Data monetization:
This is a rather new model but a model that both is high value as well as highly controversial. New legislations covering data privacy laws including the European version as the GDPR have made a lot of this clearer but also reduced the monetary potential. The overall idea of this is that it is a free platform without any commission but users giving out their data. The data itself will be sold to either allow behavior analytics, better marketing, or personal email contacts.

Aspect 4: How does your team look like for a platform business? Most start-ups start with a CEO, a CIO or head of product, a CFO, and a legal counsel. The last part has developed only lately specifically in Europe. Usually outsourced as a position, the risk of data privacy risk, data theft, and security matters has led many companies to take a more cautious aspect way of approach.
In many digital companies, the creative profiles are the drivers of products and drive business direction. Platform business is usually a much more calculated business where profiles that focus on "organization" and business model approaches drive

success. Not saying that you don't need the creative profiles for your platform business, especially for marketing, approaching clients creatively, and potentially bringing your own added value to the table you need the creative innovators, but a platform business in the purest form is an orchestrated market place where other bring the services and others buy the service while you need to make their experience easy, frictionless and optimize the process till you cannot optimize it any further.

Aspect 5: The problem of any problem is getting started. The value of a platform lies in its scale.

The more suppliers you have on your platform, the more users you will attract. The more users are on a platform the more suppliers you will attract. This is the chicken or the egg problem of the platform business. It is also the reason that YouTube videos get paid when you reach a certain number of users. The platform needs to ensure there is enough traction of content or services or products to keep the platform vital.

Most platforms focused on building a few supplier partnerships or some early content creators first to enough value in your platform before attracting users. Attracting customers can be very costly. An average CAC (customer acquisition cost) is around 400 euros for platforms varying according to industry. Which means to get 100.000 customers you will probably need to spend 4m on advertising costs.

Growing fast, do not take outside capital, reach short term profitability - Choose 1 of them.

Aspect 6: Most platforms take 7 years till they reach profitability including Airbnb was first profitable in 2018 in their 10th year, Facebook needed 3 years, Netflix 9 years reaching a profit in 2006 and Uber has not yet reached profitability.

Platforms strive to see if their potential users are numerous and their suppliers or content creators are active. Which is the reason most platforms are either global, multi-regional, or cover a complete country population? The smaller you cut your customer group the harder a platform success will become. Of course, niche platforms will take their place like in most business areas, but their potential is drastically reducing due to lower potential customers combined with a lower number of services. You might do better with targeted websites.

This might explain for example why there is not yet a cancer platform aggregating healthcare and insurance services and providing patients a 360-support system. Next to problems around stigma in some countries a key problem is that the healthcare system in every country is uniquely different, which means services as well as the regulations in each country will be distinctly different. There are very few global players that can be good partners for medical services and even items like telemedicine (video call with doctors) are not allowed for all patients worldwide. And while there the cancer is one of the top 10 death causes in the world, you only have around 2m patients in a country like Germany. Additionally, cancer is not equal to cancer. The 2m patients split over 20+ different types covering very different patient populations and patient journeys. Which is cutting down your potential target group drastically. The entry and risk barrier of this distinction and the fact that your platform needs to be adjusted for each and every individual country are a key issue. The value of scalability and speed is being prevented. This is causing many companies still to drive in the direction of owning the complete market for a certain niche holistically.

Yet this will change. Following corona and drastic pressure on the health system of most countries in the world, the health care approaches and innovations will be revolutionized. When more and more services of insurance, health companies, and tech companies become fully digital being a platform player will create opportunities. Just do not be fooled by going into the platform business, that it will be reducing your accountability as you do not own any of the products or services. It is quite the opposite. By not owning any service on the platform you have automated collective accountabilities for all the services on the platform. If an uber driver in their own car inappropriately acts towards their customers, it is Uber's accountability. If the hotel overcharges, it is booking.com's accountability to rectify. If a vendor does not deliver a product, Amazon is taking accountability.

Aspect 7: Participating in the platform game is not optional. Restaurants that do not also offer food on Deliveroo or UberEATS perform massively below the industry average. Apartments offering short term rent without Airbnb run at a lower capacity. Consumers are 89% more likely to buy a product on Amazon vs any other website.

You simply have three business strategies that each company needs to evaluate.

a) You become a platform business – where you create value focusing at aggregating the fragmented markets through connecting people and companies as frictionless as possible while taking complete accountability for success.

b) You become best at integrating your services, products into someone else's platform – where you generate value by offering your products and services in the most optimal way by identifying the right platforms early on (to get the best financial partnership deals, integrate in the most efficient way probably connecting to more than one platform, become the posterchild of a platform to gain higher revenue shares from the platform.

c) You become a unique digital niche player – You create value with a completely unique, hardly reproducible value position that makes it impossible for platforms to enter your space or over your customer group. You fill the dark spots between different platforms.

7 Things to know about Blockchain (technology group)

"Digitalizing our operations: Improving supply chain transparency through blockchain. In 2019, we tested several blockchain technologies across our dairy, nutrition, and coffee supply chains. We became the first major food company to pilot open blockchain through our collaboration with OpenSC for our Nido brands. We also worked with IBM Food Trust on our NaturNes brand to provide consumers with information relating to the product's environmental footprint. These initiatives increase traceability and transparency." Nestle Annual Report

The simplest definition of Blockchain I heard from one interviewee that I asked to explain blockchain to a child. Most others started with the discussion of private vs public, blockchain, encryption, and distributed ledger. I guess most candidates have extremely smart kids.

Yet let me share what the candidate said:

"I take a picture of Mickey Mouse and want to give it to you for 1 euro. To ensure that it is known that I give you the picture we are going to get 10 others involved.
We go to the copy machine and each of us gets a copy of this picture.
If you would then go off to a friend of yours and give him a picture of Minnie Mouse instead saying this is the original you got at the beginning, the rest of the friends(the chain) would raise their voice and mention this is not the original picture and thus prevent misuse."

More educated speaking it is a distributed ledger system.
Ledger = + and - values. Your Balance Sheet is a ledger. Your bank statement is a ledger. If somewhere a value increases somewhere else a value decreases.

Distributed = Information is stored at many places and is distributed between them. Contrary to a banking system where information is stored centrally only.

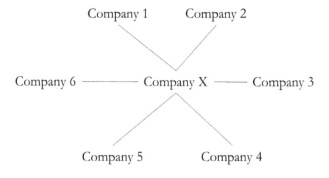

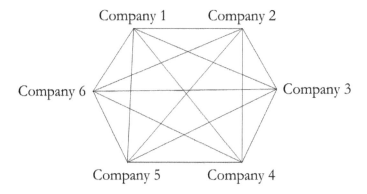

Blockchain and the cryptocurrency bitcoin is currently being attributed to a Japanese person called Satoshi Nakamoto in 2008. As bitcoin was the invention of a new currency without government supervision and without central ownership it was quickly gaining interest in various communities. The hope of transaction fee reduction that banks take for financial transfers, new transparency, and the ability to take profit and power away from banks was in the years following the financial crisis a massive attraction.

Satoshi never officially claimed he developed bitcoin largely as according to multiple law systems including the US federal law the creation of a new currency is illegal and would put any creator in prison. Officially no one knows who this person is if it is just a nickname or even a group of people.

The value of bitcoin rose as no other currency rose in many years. From 0 to 315 Euro in 2015 to 13.000 in 2017 and currently after a drop to 3.000 Euro and back to 8.700 euros in 2020. All in a currency that has neither a physical representation nor counterbalance in gold nor otherwise nor is it backed by any government or national fund. Often bitcoin, as well as blockchain, is often balancing between angel and devil. While allowing to democratize and innovate many financial processes and allow especially people with limited income to send money cost-free, it is also often used for anything in the dark web from money laundering, funding terrorist activities, drug and weapon purchases, exploiting the fact of it being an unsupervised currency.

1) There is no technology called the blockchain

Just to make things clear. There is not one "technology" as it is a concept rather than a singular technology variant. This leads to one key misunderstanding: you cannot make general statements about blockchain when you talk about strengths and weaknesses. It will strongly depend on which blockchain model you are implementing, which encryption you will be using, and how you will set up the partners. I have seen blockchains that were a blockchain just completely transparent and with horrible encryption.

2) Blockchains are not secure

The nature of blockchains allows the possibility of a higher level of security but its actual security depends on its level implementation. A low encryption blockchain is a badly secured to gain information as a low encryption non-blockchain system. Actually, it is worse in a certain way. Imagine your bank account information. All your salary information, all payments, and how much money you have. In case this information gets stolen in the past there were two potential areas for you: you were hacked, or the bank was hacked. In a blockchain environment, this problem would increase exponentially, as in case of stolen information you will have a hard time tracking where it has been stolen.

On the other hand, blockchain offers in its concept some strong security points. A blockchain allows you usually only to add information, never to delete and never to remove. Only new blocks can be added to the chain. Also, to manipulate the information you would need to hack more than 50% of the computers involved in the blockchain to be able to manipulate any content. A drastic improvement in terms of security to prevent especially a man in the middle attacks. Yet there already have been cases where loopholes in blockchain executions have been found. Your blockchain has an advantage for massive security improvements, but also a false feeling for security. The level depends on the person(s) who are implementing it.

When approaching blockchain you always have 2 key options. First, you join and surf on a public blockchain. In which case you would add your own blocks into an already existing chain and network of blockchain participants.

Alternatively, you can also build a private blockchain in which you would be able to choose the participants and it could avoid any outside access to the blockchain. It is especially in a business-to-business context relevant.

3) Blockchains are not the only way to solve problems

Not every problem is a nail for the blockchain hammer. To most, every supply chain problem became a blockchain problem (largely because of the name "chain"). Every contract needed to be converted into a smart contract.

Every problem can be solved in 100 ways and some problems could even be solved by blockchain, but just to be clear you can have a distributed ledger without blockchain, you can have a smart contract without blockchain, you could even build bitcoin without blockchain.

4) You think it makes sense to build a small blockchain with only 1 partner.

In riding trends, I saw many companies jump on the blockchain wagon. Often with issues that are neither an issue nor relevant for a blockchain problem. in 2018/2019 if you wanted your company to get investors in the tech industry you had to claim you either AI or Blockchain (preferably both) not caring if it actually makes sense. In half of the blockchain POC, companies have designed a private blockchain of 2 participants. the whole power of the blockchain lies in connecting a larger group of participants.

5) Blockchains are money based

Bitcoin is an application of a blockchain. Blockchains can be money based but do not have to be.

6) Blockchains always replace the middleman

Do not be tricked while blockchain promises to cut out the middleman, you have to be aware when working with different blockchain providers. In some cases, the blockchain creator acts as an orchestrator of the blockchain able to influence the flow of information.

7) It takes longer to develop blockchains

Only because it is new and does sound complex does not mean that it is hard to implement. Any traditional developer/IT mindset person will find that building a first blockchain application will take around 1 day. Both public as well as private. There are multiple online services, code basis and cloud supported approaches that will drastically accelerate the development. Yet quality will take time.

7 Things to remember about Quantum computing (technology group)

Once again, I will quote an explanation from one person trying to explain quantum computing. Imagine you are on the German highway with your new Mercedes. You drive 120 but there is a car in the middle lane that drives half your speed, forces you to switch lanes. You can go left or right. Which is the way basically the binary system of a computer works it allows you a 0 or 1.
Imagine you could pass the car in the middle lane at the same time left and right without splitting yourself. If you can imagine this, you have understood quantum computing.

Should you have trouble understanding this, you probably are part of the majority. Quantum computing is basically to allow that whereas today every computer is based on 0 and 1 representing on and off switches, it allows us to have switches that are both on and off at the same time.

This means we can have a computer that is faster beyond comprehension and will be an enabler of change not understandable today.

1) If you are not scared by quantum computing you have not yet understood it

The impact of quantum computing will be the next big hype.

2) It will be incomprehensible faster than before
It is already hard to imagine that today's iPhone has a higher &
faster calculation power than a room big military computer 50
years ago.
Now, imagine such a jump from 1 year to the other. That is
how scary fast this will be.
A friend of mine mentioned that today we rollout 5G and soon
we rollout 10000G on steroids.

3) It's there, it's secure, it's the only way to be scalable
Before 2023 your company will be pitched systems that are
built on quantum computing. They will not be mature yet but
you will see the starting points.

4) You will not own a QC, you will rent it via a cloud

50 years ago, when computers were massive machines and
absolutely expensive. People rented space on these machines
rather than owning. Once the cost was reduced enough people
started owning the computers and buying the hardware.
Quantum computing is at the beginning of this circle and
especially accelerated via cloud computing. Be prepared that
you will rent space very soon on a quantum computer, but not
to buy any. At least not until 2030 when owning a quantum
computer might be cheap enough for companies to own.

5) New possibilities
Quantum computing will massively drive new opportunities Ai
models with drastically improved computation power. Image
recognition, Video animation creation, cyberwar.

6) Forget today encryption.
A computer encryption today of e.g. the most sophisticated
blockchain will not take more than a few hours to crack for a
quantum computer.

We will need a completely new way of thinking around encryption.

7) Few will rule the future world
Quantum computing most likely will become the latest push that will centralize power towards a few companies. Today many different parties are able to build server farms and create cloud applications. Quantum computing is massively more expensive, yet it would attract a major market shift on the internet from many providers to a few. Considering the encryption power military will be the main customer thus allowing the first few companies global defense contracts.

7 principles of Biohacking (technology group)

Have you ever heard about BioHacking? The ability to change how your body works by embedding technology into your body to enhance it or by using substances that change your chemical behaviors or genes in your body. That is BioHacking. Sounds a bit Sci-Fi? Far from it. Using technology to change how your body works seems like a cyborg? Actually, that is what a pacemaker does or what a hearing aid implant does.
Changing your body? That is what hormone therapies do and many medicines are aimed at. Even wearables are the first part of BioHacking. Technology devices such as prosthetic arms and prosthetic legs have even helped people with disabilities lead a normal life.

BioHacking technology is defined as the flow of concepts from engineering to biology and vice versa.

When talking about BioHacking, we always split them according to 2 dimensions.

	Impacting an individual and reversible (non-invasive)	Irreversibly or Heredity impact (invasive)
Healing a defect (curing)		
Enhancing a capability (enhancing)		

One if something is enhancing your body or healing a defect. Second, if something is Invasive, meaning also your next generation is impacted by the change or if it is only impacting a single individual.

1) non-invasive – curing

In this category, you have all the tech items like pacemakers or bionic arms. Take the "Luke Skywalker" prosthetic arm. An Arm similar to that of Luke Skywalker from the star wars movies. The arms are connected to your brain and get trained to have complete motoric functionalities even bringing back a feeling of touch.

2) non-invasive – enhancing

In this category, you have everything that is making you as a person better. It includes e.g. H.U.L.C Exoskeleton which turns you into a super-soldier or bionic lenses which allows you to see like superman. Even a mind-controlling helmet that is influencing the brain activity for the better has been patented. But also, smart gloves or the apple watch can count in this category. There is an obvious grey zone at this point. In the discussion with one hearing aid company, there was an ethical discussion raised. If a person with hearing problems gets a hearing aid should we just restore his hearing to the original level, or should we allow it to be better than before?

Non-invasive but enhancing tools are often in this ethical gap. How far is too far? During the Olympics, there was a question at which point a leg replacement is an advantage too far.

3) invasive – curing

In this area, you have a lot of medicine covering gene therapy. The ability to change damaged genes in the mother or the unborn child to prevent a disease or disability. Legal in many countries even if controversial.

4) invasive - enhancing

This includes topics like DIY (do it yourself) CRISPR(clustered regularly interspaced short palindromic repeats). CRISPR is a gene-editing technology by which you can sequence and change DNA. Today you can already change your DNA via DIY kits for less than a few hundred bucks. There is a growing group of hackers that try to use DIY CRISPR to change their DNA to heal but also to enhance their lung capacity, their skin, or their longevity with massive risks. A new wave of healthcare start-ups will be created like this. Not only will medicine be created by pharma companies but moreover it will be created in garages like IT companies before. But many will pay a price on unofficial unlicensed hacks.

5) There is already a significant amount of bio hacks on the market

Many new hacks you can already buy on websites like Dangerousthings.com. (But you better not)

6) AI and automation grow at a high speed we need to adapt to keep up.

A key argument for biohacking is the need to stay up to date as a species. The technology evolutions are so fast that by not enhancing yourself we will stay behind.

7) Poor and rich will grow wider

Looking at the latest products in development at some of the start-ups it often sounds like an episode of black mirror. Yet if you look at the implications it is probably even worse. Imagine the fact that with enough money you can enhance your memory, brain capacity, physical agility, and much more. The notion of equality will be broken even further. Does it mean the need to forbid biohacking? No, it will just create a larger black market, but we need to direct the evolution towards the social good.

Evaluating your hand

Going back to your game in the Las Vegas casino. Now that we have a closer idea of what each of the technologies is, we can look at the value of our hand we had at the start of the book.

You hold a blockchain card and an artificial intelligence card in your hand. On the table is a cloud card, a digital transformation card, and a wearables card.

Card	Technology
Ace	Digitalization
King	Platform
Queen	AI
Jack	Cloud
10	Wearables
9	Digital Transformation
8	ERP
7	Blockchain
6	Chatbots
5	AR / VR
4	RPA
3	Bio-Hacking
2	Quantum Computing

This would mean that today with the hand you are holding, you basically hold a Queen and a 7 while on the table you have a Jack, a 9, and a 10. Not bad hand but not the best either.

And unfortunately compared to the timeless game of poker, the value of the cards is changing over time. While digitalization was an ACE at the time of corona it will lose more and more relevance as a differentiator. It will become a foundation, nevertheless. On the other hand, digital transformation, platforms, and AI will become the dominating technology drivers over the next 10 years.

Yet as we said, the action happens in the next cycle the new trend technologies will become biohacking and quantum computing. Blockchain will be a good investment but far below the expectation levels seen today.

Card	Technology 2020	Technology 2024	Technology 2028
Ace	Digitalization	Platform	Digital Transformation
King	Platform	AI	Platform
Queen	AI	Wearables	AI
Jack	Cloud	Digitalization	Bio-Hacking
10	Wearables	Digital Transformation	Quantum Computing
9	Digital Transformation	Cloud	Blockchain
8	ERP	Blockchain	Cloud
7	Blockchain	AR / VR	Wearables
6	Chatbots	Bio-Hacking	AR / VR
5	AR / VR	Quantum Computing	Digitalization
4	RPA	Chatbots	Chatbots
3	Bio-Hacking	ERP	ERP
2	Quantum Computing	RPA	RPA

Strategy to change your odds

If we have a good high-level understanding of which cards we have and what they are worth as well understand the overall game we are playing, we reach a stage where the next step is to improve the odds of us winning. Especially the digital transformation that can enable massive disruptions in your ecosystem, can gain exponentially from every percentage of improving the failure rate. To do this we are going to next look at what typical failure lessons are, what key success factors are, and how you can utilize them.

What do companies do that win on their digital transformation journey?

It was a question that bothered me quite a bit. I spend time in analyzing how certain companies succeed where others are just running in constant circles.

First, I wanted to analyze what impact organizational structure, as well as governance, have.
Was there maybe prove that had certain company structures are more successful or less successful than others? Would a top-down structure support digital transformation more than a bottom-up structure? Or would a freedom model like google bring the digital drive with it?
Unfortunately, all data I had proved that structure is a low-quality predictor for digital success. In my study as many top-down as bottom-up companies failed at the transformation. As many companies with separate digital team vs integrated digital team have been successful. As many strong governance companies as well as low governance/freedom companies failed and succeeded.

This is echoing other types of transformations from cultural transformations within the company to political transformations.
We must see the organization structure simply as the playing field that we have to play each time according to its rules.

No organization or structure prevents transformation but also no structure automatically enables transformation, neither positive nor negative.
Take the most extreme example of a country transformation: dictatorships. A significant amount of dictatorships started as democratic models. As you might remember that Caesar, Mussolini, and especially Hitler were all democratically elected either to lead their party or to lead the country.
Organizational structure, governance structures, and hierarchical structures are not irrelevant in a transformation but are a lesser item to consider.

Instead what was recurring is that out of 10 companies that I before classified as successful digital transformation companies 9 talked about leadership, specifically digital leadership, or leadership in a digital age.
And as we saw before out of the companies that in my study failed, 3 key issues were repeatedly mentioned: Leadership, Communication, and Strategy.

The first curious thing is that in no cases technology was ever mentioned. The second curious thing is that it seems the key issues of digital transformation are the same as any transformation idea and even that these aspects transcend age as they were key aspects of each failed monarchy, each successful revolution, and any successful company in history. Ranging from Roman times to Napoleon to Oliver Cromwell & Queen Elisabeth and the American independence to today. The third curious thing is the order of the three first came Leadership, second communication, and third strategy.

What makes a good digital leader?

If we look at each of the items and we start with leadership, the first question that comes to mind is what or who are great leaders. Obviously, each culture has its own perspective on what great leadership is, so I used the world's most representative way of getting information: Google. Concretely by searching "Who are great Leaders" on google.de (in German), google.com (in English), google.ru (in Russian). The results were as following:

US: Nelson Mandela, Gandhi, Steve Jobs, Martin Luther King, Lincoln, JFK, Bill Gates, Churchill, Napoleon

Germany: Jeff Bezos, Christine Lagarde, Jack Ma, Howard Schultz, Tim Cook, Pope Francis, Merkel, Aung San Suu Kyi

Russia: Genghis Khan, Martin Luther King, Papa Gregory, Lenin, Jeanne d'Arc, Oliver Cromwell, Napoleon, Tsar Vladimir, Pieter First

7 key differentiators of a good (digital) leader

I found 7 key differentiators and the good thing is each of these can be learned. It does not matter the type of company, the age of your employees or

Differentiator 1: They have a Vision

The general who wins the battle makes many calculations in his temple before the battle is fought. The general who loses makes but few calculations beforehand - Sun Tzu

---

Transformation without vision and hoping only for opportunistic successes is like playing soccer but you put the blindfolds on for your team. You might shoot a goal through individual efforts, but you will not succeed long term.

When there is no vision, people perish — Roosevelt

Transformation without a vision is just wasted effort.
Changing without focus uses all its company energy in pulling in different directions. Becoming digital "is not a good vision.
"being the best digital company" is not a good vision.
"Having the best technology" is not a good vision.
You want to be clear about how digital helps you and your customer. In principle, your vision needs to be easy to read and remember.

A vision needs to be focused on customer obsession. Leaders start with customer needs. They focus on building trust and pay attention to the competition but obsess over the customers. They are obsessed with just the competition not just their personal gains.

Every leader with a strong vision accepts things long before they become mainstream. They recognize internal and external inventions. Opposed you see many B grade leaders talk down innovations that did not come from their own team. But most successful leaders see the trends early on. As you need to be confident to be humble, the same way you need to be confident in your vision to be able to be a humble leader.
The highest value generation happens on the next innovation cycle. It is about being early on the next trend, not the last trend. Great leaders identify these trends faster than others and structure their vision around the future.
A great vision needs to commit to a unique value proposition and in the digital age "price" is getting a less and less important factor. Go big or go home is becoming a more and more relevant motto in the digital world. Due to the low cost of entering markets going big is as possible as going for a niche.

Differentiator 2: Playing towards strength

If you talk well - use it. If you are the innovator - use it. If you are the best organizer - use it. Leaders that focus on improving their weakness always led to mediocrity. Only if you play towards your strength, you will reach new heights.

Differentiator 3: Risk-taking, Persistence

Take positivity out of failure. Others around you will discourage you and you will be told that there is nothing to gain from doing what you do. Great leaders take advice but also take risks and persist to go in the direction where the wind is going. If their dream takes them upriver, then this is where they go. They believe it before they see it.

Failure is the opportunity to begin again more intelligently" - Henry Ford

---

Always remember as a leader that around innovation every expert is clueless. "There is no reason why anyone would want a computer in their home", Ken Olsen. "The telephone has too many shortcomings to be seriously considered. The device has no value to us. ", Western union 1876. "I think there is a world market of maybe 5 computers.", Thomas Watson, Chairman of IBM in 1943.

Differentiator 4: Leaders commit and deliver results

Digital Leaders show extreme ownership. They disagree and commit. They own mistakes and they own successes. They act on behalf of the entire organization, not their own individual teams. They have a different perception of time as they never sacrifice the future for the present. They look at the past, the present and the future equally balanced. In digital companies you usually have the CEO demoing the products and tools.
And most important they get things done. Digital is fast. Digital is speed. By discussing for a month what to do a select idea you might already be outdated and have been bypassed by a 16-year-old in some part of the world. Great leaders have a bias for action and follow their instincts.

In the digital casino, you will always be given some cards. You have two options. A) Play the cards you are dealt with.

B) If you do not like the rules, find a way to change the game. Digital leaders excel at knowing when to follow the rules and when to change the game.

Differentiator 5: Leaders are surrounded by great people

They hire and develop the best. Every hire needs to be better than the last. They recognize exceptional talent and they are willing to move them through the organization. A-players hire A+ players, B-players hire C-players. You can identify leadership often by the fact if they hire the best people. Weak leaders look for people that cannot endanger their position.

Each leader has people around them that make the success happen. Steve Jobs had Steve Woznick. Napoleon had Michel Nay. Queen Elisabeth had Sir Francis Walsingham.
Leaders need to be surrounded by great people to become great. No one can change the world alone.
Great leaders also know when to let go of people. When to cut loose negative people or pure complainers. Complaining is a disease that destroys projects, transformations, companies, and whole governments.

They also insist on the highest standards. Many see their standards being set as unreasonable yet keeping raising the bar will drive higher quality products, project success, innovation, and agility. They tackle elephants at the point they occur.

The best leaders transverse all levels and earn trust by listening attentively, speaking candid, and treat others respectfully.

Differentiator 6: Design & Language count

A vision needs to be remembered; it is the first impression you make on others. Great digital leaders understand that the design of the product, messaging and brand is an important part of your value proposition. Psychology gives us a few tips in this area.

a) Follow the Trinity:
To make it rememberable we want to follow the trinity. Remember the "Veni, Vidi, Vici" of Caesar, "Faster, higher, stronger" of the Olympics, or "liberty, equality, fraternity" of the French Revolution.
The rule of three is one of the most powerful concepts in writing, speaking, and advertisement. Aristotle said that each story should have a start, a middle, and an ending. You have the three musketeers and three pigs. The declaration of independence ensures three basic rights. Neuroscientists often proved that humans would digest information better when presented in threes. Tim Cook while introducing the Apple Watch introduced it as "breakthrough technology, powerful software and world-class service" and it will help people to "stay connected, be more active and live a healthier life".

You might also remember the first time this was keenly noticed that Apple was focused on the rule of three in 2007 when Steve Jobs introduced the iPhone buy saying he will present three new revolutionary products.
"A widescreen iPod with touch controls, a revolutionary mobile phone, and a breakthrough internet communication device. These are not three separate devices; this is one device and we call the iPhone."

b) Use repetition:
"We shall fight them on the beaches, we will fight them on the landing grounds, we shall fight them on the field and in the streets. we shall never surrender". We need repetition. Marketing is effective because of repetition.

c) Metaphors are verbal beauty: AI winter. Arabic spring. Digital lifeblood. Data is the new oil.

Metaphors stay in the head where other information will be lost.

d) Make it rhyme:
- No app no Map - Introducing google maps
- Our company will create an original digital
- Welcome to visual digital
- Artificial intelligence creating decision relevance
- Apply AI to reach the Sky
- Transformation Education Innovation
- Analysis Paralysis
- Data Science Alliance
- Breath-taking Decision making
- No more faking decision making

e) Use slogans
You probably remember slogans like "Because I'm worth it" or "Impossible is nothing" or "Just do it".
A lot of these slogans depend on your personality, culture, and personal preference but my personal favorite digital slogans were:
- Right decision. Right moment. Right place. - Every time! (when introducing Augmented decision making through AI)
- The power to change the world - at your fingertip. (introducing a writing app)
- Your phone is digital. Your car digital. Your money digital. But your business does not need to change? (digital transformation consulting company)
- If you wait it is too late (advertising change)

More than just the slogan your digital vision should frame how the future looks like for customers, company, and employees. Every employee. The clearer your vision and the proposal for each stakeholder are the better the vision will translate.

Differentiator 7: Leaders are great storytellers

Communication is the key to change. The best products are worth nothing if no one understands them. Your vision is worth nothing if your team can't understand it. Storytellers in ancient times were the most exciting revered people in the world. Rhetoric and storytelling are some of the best attributes of leaders today.

(Checklist) for a great digital leader

- ☐ Leaders are great storytellers
- ☐ They make Design & Language count
- ☐ Leaders commit and deliver results
- ☐ A-class player hire +A-class players
- ☐ Leaders are surrounded by great people
- ☐ Let go of complainers
- ☐ Digital leaders excel at knowing when to follow the rules and when to change the game.
- ☐ Risk-taking, Persistence
- ☐ Playing towards one's strength
- ☐ Have a Vision
- ☐ Embrace internal and external ideas
- ☐ Great leaders repeat, repeat, repeat

What makes a good digital communication?

Our lives are a summary of thousands of stories. As humans, we are predetermined to be influenced by stories. Religions were spread by telling stories long before holy books were shared among the commons. The 8 lessons of Buddha. The 10 commandments. There is only a certain amount of information we can process and the easier it is shared with us the more we can remember. Luther's 99 thesis was only able to be shared after the book printing started and reading was becoming more and more common.

We go to movies and spend hours watching imaginary stories. We love it. We binge days' worth of Netflix of romance, action, and drama. Stories are an integral part of our lives in any century. Advertisements are short stories. The more we can connect to the stories told the more likely we are to buy a certain product or act in a certain way. We are not convinced by facts but by how the facts are being presented. Today rhetoric, communication skills, and speeches have a strong impact on society. Persuasion is responsible for 25% of American income. Persuasion is universal, every industry needs it. Every leader needs it. Every parent needs it. Entrepreneurs persuade investors to back start-ups. Candidates persuade recruiters. Leaders persuade employees to take specific actions. Salespersons persuade customers. Politicians lie.

Except for the last one we have much to gain by learning storytelling. Let us learn from two great storytellers from very different generations: Aristotle and Pixar.

In ancient Greece, rhetoric was held as a privilege to influence the masses. Aristotle was viewed as a thorn in the side of the Greek ruling class. He wanted rhetoric to be accessible by all classes. So, he shared his wisdom on great storytelling with the world.

350 BC Aristotle has given us a few hints on how to improve communication and storytelling. He looked at a few key features:

- Ethos or establish the author's credibility or character: You must prove that you are trustworthy, credible, and worth listening too. Which includes fair or unbiased communication as well as introducing your expertise
- Logos or why should the audience care about your idea. It is about Data, facts, or evidence. You use logic to connect and convince your audience
- Pathos / Emotion. Make people feel; you try to trigger a neurochemical reaction in the brain to drive their emotions to get their buy-in and emotional connection to the story
- Less is always more. Humans can only absorb so much information
- By using the combination of the three above with the limitation of less is more you can generate influential speeches & stories

Fast forward 2300 years and let us take a look at how Pixar has evolved from the few principles to a higher-end ideology for great storytelling.

Principle 1: Great stories are simple and focused
Not each story we tell needs to be Agatha Christie level with a variety of twists and turns. Most great stories are simple. Toy story is still one of the most entertaining and engaging but not the most unpredictable storyline. At every point during it, you are knowing what is happening, there is no confusion. Its simplicity and focus itself are so exhilarating.
As storyteller especially in business we want to include as much information as possible, but most people's attention span is tiny. You want to bring your point. Make it simple and focused.

Principle 2: Great stories are surprising

Simplicity does not mean a story cannot have turned. Any surprises will create suspense and interest.

In business that can mean you change the way, you present what you want to present. Do not use the typical slide deck. How about making a movie instead of a slide? Add a surprising slogan. Look at presentations of apple every 14 min a new presenter or change in presentation method (e.g. Video) is happening.

Principle 3: Great stories touch us emotionally and intellectually

In principle we are ruled by 6 basic emotions: Anger, Disgust, Fear, Happiness, Sadness, and Surprise.

Continuously ask yourself what are you feeling when thinking about the topic of your story and why? Once you know it, use the why to extrapolate your feeling on the audience.

A great story connects to their audience on intellectual and emotional levels.

Principle 4: Great stories have a character you want that he/she/it wins at the end

Everyone wants to root for the underdog. Everyone wants a hero. You want your company to be what people are rooting for. Your project wants to be the underdog. Play with this feeling.

Principle 5: Great stories have a purpose

Why do YOU tell THIS story? What does it TEACH? What great PURPOSE does it supply?

Answer the questions and you will make your story even more driven.

Principle 6: great stories are universal

Sometimes we think about a great argument in a discussion or an amazing joke but once we tell it only 2 or 3 people laugh or react. The idea of a great story needs to be so fundamental that it transcends culture, opinions, and time.
It shall be universal and should resonate with as many people as possible. The key is to know your own voice and be aware of your own feelings about the story you are going to tell.

Principle 7: great stories come in every length

Stories can be long or short.

"Baby shoes to sell - unused"

Or

"On his gravestone: Don't try"

No garden is perfect until you cannot remove anything from it anymore. Make sure your story has everything it needs but nothing more.

(Checklist) for a great story

- ☐ What is the essence of the story?
- ☐ What is interesting for the audience is not what is interesting for the storyteller
- ☐ Rewrite your stories
- ☐ Clear structure
- ☐ Simplify, focus, jump over detours
- ☐ What are the story characters strength - how would they overcome the exact opposite situation
- ☐ Have the ending clear before you reach the middle
- ☐ Let go even if it is not perfect
- ☐ Character need opinions
- ☐ Understand: Why must you tell this story
- ☐ Imagine you in that situation - honesty lends credibility to situations
- ☐ What are the stakes to root for the character?
- ☐ Coincidence is never the solution
- ☐ You got to identify with the situation

What makes a good digital strategy?

We reached the point where we have discussed digital leadership as well as great communication & storytelling. Next, we will look at the even more difficult part. Your strategy in digital.

Strategy without tactics is the slowest route to victory. Tactics without strategy are the noise before defeat. - Sun Tzu

---

"Strategy" is a term that originated in the military. It descends from the Greek word of strategia. Meaning generalship or commanding an army. Army strategy was focused on how to use resources (human and otherwise) effectively and establish a favorable position.

The biggest problem for companies around digital is that they do not have a strategy covering digital or if they do, they have a strategy that starts from the wrong angle. Most failed "digital strategies" start from the technology. Yet the goal of such a strategy is not to work on the best technology but generate the best possible value. Do not ever mistake a technology roadmap for a digital strategy and understand that serendipity is not a strategy.

A strategy is about making choices; It is about deliberately choosing to be different

---

Strategies are focused on coordination. Strategies are surprising. Strategies make sure to take the right steps at the right time.

To create a strategy there are two key frameworks: the traditional strategy model, and the strategy Ikigai. Both are similar but have a few differentiating factors.

According to the traditional strategy model, every strategy in battle or business needs to define 4 items.

- Where (in which space) do we compete, which includes geographical location, customers, customer-facing business model ecosystem and positioning
- What unique value do we bring, which includes what are our key strength and what makes us special to gain the space in which we compete
- What resources/capabilities do we utilize, which includes employees, skills, financials, or other assets
- How do we sustain unique value, which is focused on the long-term unique value proposition (UVP), long term sustainability, and how to ensure others are not overcoming our UVP?

The Ikigai strategy model is based on the Japanese self-development model. Later in the book, we will look deeper into this model's history, but for the time being, the Ikigai strategy building approach answers 4 different questions:

- **What are you good at?** In other words, your unique value proposition. What makes your company/department special? What do you have that others do not have? Where are you different from others?
- **What does the world need?** What problem do you solve? Who are your customers and what value do they get from you?

- **What do you get paid for?** What is your business model? How do you sustain your long-term success?
- **What do you enjoy?** While this does not sound like a company strategy question it is a metaphor for the company culture, change management, and organizational shift. It is about how do you mobilize your workforce to focus on your customer and maximize the value proposition. It is about what is your work culture that will enable. It is about what drives your employees to come to work for you and what your employer value proposition is. It is the question of why any talent work for you would.

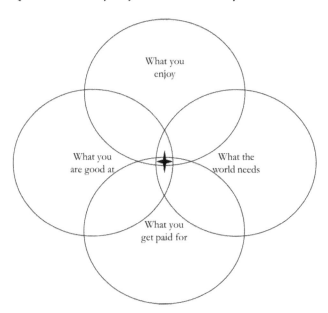

If you do not have all four aspects, you will end up in a less favorable position than you could have been. Ikigai means for a simplicity purpose: What it is worth to get up in the morning for. For business, it means: **What is your reason for being.** The Ikigai strategy, if successful applied places you in a state of balance and prepares you for success.

You will as a company fail if you have a business model that you are not good at. You will fail if you cover a need in the world but can't make many to sustain your business. You will fail if you have something you are good at but you are losing key employees and can't attract great ones because you miss a good employer value proposition.

The second part of the definition of digital strategy is the specialization of digital. Every good digital strategy is derived from the business strategy, encompasses culture, organization, digital technology, and has the customer at heart.

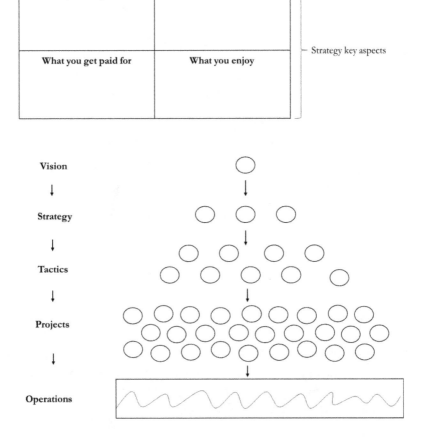

Having the customer at heart sounds easy but it is a fine line between creating value for your customer and listening blindly to your customer.

The best advice I ever got on this was:

Listen to your customer's needs - do not listen to what your customer wants

People do not know what they want nor is it their job to know. Instead, listen to what their needs are and propose solutions which you reiterate till you hit the target.

Take an example from a company I worked with:

"We spend a lot of time in one painful administration process. When we asked people how to improve, they asked for a chatbot to enter the admin in the system and lead the customer thorough the difficult processes.

Not a bad idea but if we look at the real need, it is getting the admin done with minimal effort and limited knowledge needs at high accuracy. So instead, we decided to predict the admin entries and eliminate the needs for all manual processes related to it. Everything now is booked automatically with exception management. Faster, better, cheaper, and higher value but not what people originally asked for"

Ask people what they want, and they will say faster horses - Henry Ford

Henry Ford said: "Ask people what they want, and they will say faster horses." While I am not a fan of the cars of Ford, I believe that this is one of the most underestimated statements in the world. It describes a key issue. No one knows what they want and those that do, cannot explain it to others.

We are very good at describing the status quo yet struggle at changing our viewpoint to explain what we want.

There are 3 explanations for that
1) We cannot communicate what we want
2) We think the solution not the problem
3) We simply do not know what we do not know

1) We cannot communicate what we want?
And I do not mean the problem that developers and customers rarely speak the same language but rather the simple fact that what makes sense in your head, does not make sense for most others. Have you ever had the experience where something that sounded super smart in your head was sounding stupid once you said it? Or that an idea you had that was for you clear as glass but no one in the room got you? It is unfortunately a natural phenomenon. Your brain simplified a lot of connections and you barely know a small percent of why you came to certain ideas. Let me take you through a couple of examples. It's a rainy day, it has been pouring for days, you are spending a large amount of time on your sofa staring out the window, hoping for change. Your children are running around, playing with their Lego less and less, and are more and more anxious. One day your child asks you: "When will the rain stop?" Partially annoyed you react by saying "probably end of the week", while the truth is that you have no clue.

If we take a step back, do we believe the child just wanted to know when it will stop raining? What is the question behind the question and what is the problem our child has?
There is a good chance that our child is most likely more interested when it can play outside again and run more or play hide and seek in the garden rather than wonder about the empirical evolution of meteorology. One of the key aspects of

the collection of needs is that you always look for actionability. If you give answers or build solutions, how do they lead to actions?

Can anyone take action on the weather in this situation of our little family? So rather than going into predicting the weather it might be more relevant to completely readjust the furniture in the house and build an adventure park where your child is enjoying life despite the outside weather.

During the corona crisis, many colleagues told me they want the lockdown to stop. I often asked them one simple question: Why? What do they miss? I cannot change the lockdown but maybe I can help them find ways on how to make the situation better. It is better than swelling on the annoying idea of being stuck in a room and how hard life is.

Some were concerned about the lack of human contact, so we discussed how to use more video chats and virtual coffee breaks to connect or to have 1-1 discussions in a part of the city center.

Some were annoyed by cooking, so we discussed which food delivery has the most unique food.

Some were worried about their job, so we discussed how we can change the situation.

The key is that you figure out the real problem of what people are saying or asking. It is a long process to get to the right "why", which you should not short cut others are stuck in a problem vs solution dead-end.

2) Solution vs problem

If you interview people or collect people's needs in any other way, you should never ask people what they think the solution is until way down the line. Only once you deeply understand their problem, they can join the journey of finding a solution. Too often I have seen that people explain not what they need but what they want. Which led to the paradox that even if you give them exactly what they want, they do not need it.

3) We simply do not know what we do not know.

An obvious statement but I believe 90% of readers (and myself as well) have been in this state at more than one of their projects. Steve Jobs could have asked one million people and probably no one would have said I need an iPad, or I need a social network to Facebook before they knew it exists.

These are also the reasons why innovative solutions should never be explained to focus groups until you have a prototype. Any focus group you do before the prototype stage is burned money.

What is Ikigai for your digital strategy & digital flow?

If we structure our digital strategy going back to Ikigai, it is structured around the 4 principle questions. Each of the principles has a few sub-items to consider.

What you are good at:
As this section talks about your overall company strength as well as your digital strength it contains what you are good at as well as what you will be good at, in contrast to an individual's Ikigai you can exchange parts of the organization to get new parts or acquire/merge with other organizations.

It must be derived from your overall business strategy and covers overarching strengths including product positioning, brand benefits, etc.

In other words, the unique value proposition. If you are good at design, it needs to be a key driver for your digital products & projects. When you are great at the aggregating fragmented market it needs to be the key driver in your digital strategy including your digitally enhanced business model. When you have experts in your company around AI use them no matter what position they have.

What you get paid for:
In short, the business model. How do you use the resources you have to create more value than you spend resources? Business models range from creating marketplaces to digital solutions that provide new revenue streams via direct sales or advertising or by increasing existing sales by enhancing a product value proposition. The most interesting part about digital is that it challenges traditional business model concepts & key assumptions.

Company value is disconnected from their assets:
Take the Platform Enterprise. Companies or products that aggregate fragmented markets. Airbnb, Uber, Facebook, YouTube. Companies that do not own any assets but connect consumers and companies most efficiently. Uber does not own any care or Airbnb does not own any apartments. YouTube does not create any videos.

Your cost (cost of sales) does not increase with the number of customers.
Take the Infinite Enterprise. In digital, scalability is everything. To the point that software and service development costs per customer almost reach zero (100% profitability for each one). Waze, the app that uses real-time traffic information coming in from users worldwide in a co-creation model, at zero cost, and using social media to make the information viral. In digital is exponential at non-exponential cost. If 10 users or 100.000 use the app the cost is the same.

Pricing & offers are dynamic and faster than humanly possible to understand.
The Real-Time Enterprise involves getting and applying real-time learning (Real-Time Data Feedback) when it gathers and analyses massive data sources that let it optimize its product offer, price, and quantity throughout the entire lifecycle. You can create offers and pricing updates at a speed that is hard to comprehend. High-speed trading algorithms are now

responsible for more than half of Wall Street trading. With one AI running over 10.000 trades per second.

Personalization is a low-cost high value add.
You see the rise of the Intimate Enterprise: Personalisation as the norm. Creating optimal experiences and solutions for each customer comes at a low cost but allows a major boost in a value proposition.
Take Spotify, where they use algorithms to offer content consumption recommendations based on data and recommendations from other users, and consolidated habits.

What the world needs:
Your digital strategy needs to be anchored in your "why". What does the world need? Why does your company/digital strategy exist? What gap in the world do you address?
The „why"is a lot more difficult to define for most companies than expected. If you go to google translate and to translate for example the German sentence you will get a surprising result.

(German) „Was ist der Unterschied zwischen wieso, weshalb, warum, weswegen, darum, deshalb, deswegen? „

(English) "What is the difference between why, why, why, why, why, why, why"

Your "why" is a complex multi-dimensional item.
Why are you doing DIGITAL? Why are YOU doing digital? How is your ecosystem evolving and what new needs are being generated?

Makes sure it has a high ambition level but a strong focus. Energy flows where focus goes.

What you enjoy:
This part is mostly on your company culture, your values, and what drives you. Digital must be an amplifier in your culture, not a contradiction. While at the same time you need to invest in a new mindset. Digital means Ambiguity as a constant. Digital means you need an agile attitude. In this section, you need to also explain your unique value proposition towards EMPLOYEES. Why should great talents work for you?

(Check List) Digital strategy

- ☐ **Do you have a circular balanced portfolio between digitalization, digital transformation, and digital enablers?**
- ☐ **Is it part or derived from the overall company strategy?**
- ☐ **What are you good at?** your unique value proposition. What makes your company/department special? What do you have that others do not have?
- ☐ **What does the world need?** What problem do you solve? Who are your customers and what value do they get from you?
- ☐ **What do you get paid for?** What is your business model? How do you sustain your long-term success? Did you consider new digital adjusted business model assumptions?
- ☐ **What do you enjoy?** It is about how do you mobilize your workforce to focus on your customer and maximize the value proposition. It is about what is your work culture that will enable. It is about what drives your employees
- ☐ **Do you have a Data & digital literacy index?**
- ☐ **What is your digital ethical framework?**
- ☐ **Is the strategy ambitious but focused?**
- ☐ **Is your strategy written from a customer & employee point of view?**
- ☐ **Is it containing the competency and mindset change chapter?**
- ☐ **Do you have a data tactics appendix?**
- ☐ **Is your strategy connected to incentives?**
- ☐ **What do you NOT do?**

Data & digital literacy index

Companies today are great at processing data. We process data like we do process oil. But most oil that exists is a gift by Mother Earth. Data is either auto-generated like GPS signals of your phone or entered by a human. A few years back you had "data entry jobs", who were completely focused on ensuring we enter data from forms into our systems. Today there are very few of these jobs, rather they have merged with many other jobs as part of the day to day activities.

A sales rep is not only selling but maintaining CRM systems, call logs, answering surveys, and validates financial admin questions. We did amazing jobs at preparing the data flows but missed a key item. We add work for individuals without them gaining any benefits from. And as for every topic if there is no value for you to do something you either don't do it or you spend the least amount of time. Most people don't understand the value of entering data in systems or what is the impact of having the wrong data in the systems?

Defense data tactics will be working on quality as an enabler. The best to improve the quality of data is to have the right data in the systems from the beginning. To reach that everyone needs to understand why they enter what for what reason.

- Data literacy is the ability to read, interpret, create at the right quality level, and communicate data as contextualized insights.
- Digital literacy is the ability to understand, interact, utilize, design our digital environment to its fullest value potential

Data & digital literacy are both a combination of mindset as well as competency as well as a measurement instrument. In most companies' literacy is calculated via online assessments using a standardized test or manager assessment of each employee to then calculate how many people are already literate in that domain.

Evaluation per Employee	Digital Literacy Rating	Data Literacy Rating
25% - 50%	Aware of the digital environment.	Understands the defense strategy and the importance of defending data
50% - 75%	Understand the digital environment Understands how to use digital to improve	Understands the attack strategy and can use data, insights, etc to its maximum
75% - 100%	Able to design and influence the digital environment. Ability to disrupt the ways of work and the environment	Ability to design data orchestration, data tactics, and data utilization

Data Literacy Index
$$= \frac{Employees\ with\ a\ data\ rating\ above\ 50\%}{Employees\ with\ a\ data\ rating\ below\ 50\%}$$

Digital Literacy Index
$$= \frac{Employees\ with\ a\ digital\ rating\ above\ 50\%}{Employees\ with\ a\ digital\ rating\ below\ 50\%}$$

Tactics to win the game

"Strategy requires thought, tactics require observation" – Max Euwe

---

Finally, we are going to look at a set of smaller and larger tactics you can employ. Each of these tactics covers **how,** while your strategy defines **what & why**. If we take the analogy of our card game of the beginning, the tactics help you will win each hand, whereas your strategy helps you to win the game and leave at the right moment.

A few tactics we have already seen in earlier chapters like the TYR (transformative yet recognizable), the business question rephrasing, technology capitalization, or the circular portfolio but let us put them into the right context to see how they fit. None of the tactics will help you if you do not have a good strategy, but they will help you ease the way to a higher level of success.

Taking better decisions than the competition	Data as an Asset Game Theory Be where others are not Accuracy vs explainability Digital Ethics
Efficiency & effectiveness	No-touch – low touch Extra value processes design Agile technology landscapes
Right resources at the right place	Circular Portfolio Business question rephrasing Where focus goes energy flows Aggregate vs defragment markets Innovation & Disciplined agility Innovate to negotiate Next cycle
The best solution	TYR Digital Design Wins Digital scalability Change management hacks
Creating high performing teams	Recruitment Revolution Roles of the Future Ikigai & Strength Theory Digital Identity
Across all	Digital Technology Capitalisation Creation through recombination

(Tactic) Data as an Asset, the infinite problem

A lens of each digital strategy is data tactics. The ability to capitalize and monetize your data by informing decisions improving ways of working or helping product design is needed for every transformation. Data tactics are not new. Your IT department probably has some for a long time. Yet the relevance of the scale and the aspects are changing. Future data tactics will need to include a few new concepts like enlightened data, expiry of information, attack data vs defense data tactics, data literacy, and quality index.

Data is everywhere. In your company, you sit on such a massive amount of data. Yet in your data tactics and your mind, you think only about 10% of all data.

You think about excels, sales, numbers. Do not forget that every email, every word document is data. Every website produces data. Every time you use your ID at each gate at work you generate data.

Your data tactics need to encompass all data not just 10% of easily structured data.

Here you start stepping into an infinite problem. You need to create data to explain data that requires new management. Acknowledging that you are facing an infinite problem is already a must. We need to recognize that we cannot tackle an infinite problem with finite approaches. The way we want to control data access, growth & sharing is unfortunately not scalable. You can create the best network of data owners, governance & data warehouses and will still only manage to improve by a few percents.

We must fundamentally rethink our defense & our attack tactics.

Let me try to paint you a picture of this. The way we handle data today is by trying to put it into different boxes and organize them in a warehouse. Yet we reached a stage where data is more like a river(not a lake, as a lake is not moving while data is constantly in transit). Good luck trying to put a river into boxes.
You can't count, order, or categorize parts of the river, but you can guide it by making sure the right frame is placed. Just don't try to block too much of the river, it will find its way around.

In your data tactics, the defense data tactics are all about how to secure, access, limited liabilities, store effectively and at a right quality level,
Attack data tactics are about how you utilize, monetize, and capitalize to generate value.

One example switch is the concept of enlightened data.

Enlightened Data Vs Dark Data

Have you heard friends or colleagues saying data is the new gold? Only that you can share it and it does not lose its value? This is very true but unfortunately, the meaning of what is behind this is being interpreted in very different ways and used mostly out of context.

And here is one more challenge for you: I want you to think about how data for you looks like.

If in your mind you know see either an excel file or something similar like a database, I would ask you to think one step further and ask yourself if data would not look like this how could it be looking like.

To go behind this, we will need to look at two types of data: Dark Data and Enlightened Data.
Dark data is what we are used to, the datasets at work, the excel sheets with customer information, etc. Yet the data is almost exclusively without connection and context.

Over the last 30 years, brilliant systems have been built to store relevant data and minimize any unnecessary connection in data storage. It was needed as the storage space was massively limited and the calculation power of computer way below the current capabilities of even a smart fridge or an Apple Watch. Therefore, storage software vendors build tools and modeling approaches to reduce the maximum size of data that is being recorded. One of the key aspects of was for example data normalization invented by Edgar F Codd. This was explored as three normal forms of data and focused on build primary data key, secondary keys, splitting data sets into atomic data points. Unnecessary entries were removed. Unless necessary, data points could be disconnected or removed entirely. E.g. very few systems ever recorded, who entered data or changed data - none measure why the data was entered or in which situation the person who entered the data was. Enlightenment data means contextualized, accurate, timely, and relevant.

Let us take the example of you having a bottle in front of you. Your data is that it is a glass bottle filled with orange juice that you received 3 days ago. Which action would you take from this information? Would you drink? Why not?

The context that is missing that the oranges produced are sprayed with pesticides and was presented to you by your son who hates your guts and wants your inheritance. Would you still take the same action?

The data does not change, the context of it did. The impact is drastic.

How does this look in the data management world?

If I have a data file that contains the number of 1234 this a perfect example of dark data. You have one or many data points in a file but these data points have no value until you know that it is my pin code for my card that it will expire in 2 months, and that is linked to the customer reward system of 11 hotel chains. The additional context will tell you that I selected the number because I was lazy or because I have issues remembering things.

In the past, we visualize data storage as tables, sometimes as cubes. Enlightened data is forcing a new way of storing data. Then it moved into cubes in systems like SAP BW or comparable data storage systems. Future data yet will become spherical. Imagine a tennis ball where every millimeter is a data point that is collected to every other data next to it and above and below it. With the most connected data points in the center of the tennis ball.

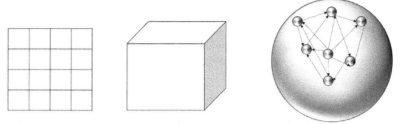

If you take any data set and you connect each data point to each of the data points in the data set that it has the connection what happens is that every time you generate a sphere.

What happens if you add a second dataset which itself is also a sphere. Initially, we assumed that it would become a network of connected spheres, but with every dataset, we found that instead, it becomes a large sphere. If you add two spheres of the same size, they will create a sphere that is 1.41 its original size. If you add a sphere with another sphere that is 2 times its size the combined sphere will grow to 1.72 of the largest spheres.

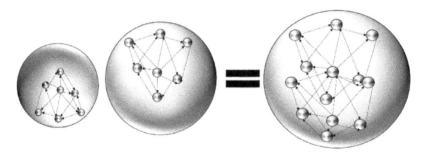

The more enlightened your data is the denser your data sphere will become. This allows us to measure contextualization as Sphere density over the sphere number of volume (data points).

$$\text{Data Contextualisation} = \frac{Sphere\ density}{Sphere\ volume}$$

Meaning if you have a dataset with 10 data points your maximum density would be 10x10 connections resulting in a density of 100 over 10, which represents a complete sphere meaning your data is contextualized with each value data point you have.

If in the same setting you would only have 2x10 connections resulting in a density of 20 over 10 it will give you the indication that you are probably missing data in the data set.

To reach a contextualized dataset you will need a number of data points to root 6 as the number of connections.

$$\min \text{Enlightenment index} \ = \ \sqrt[6]{Number\ of\ data\ points}$$

If you have a dataset of
- 100 data points you will need in average 2.15 connections per data point
- 10.000 data points you will need in average 4.64 connections per data point
- 1.000.000 data points you will need in average 10 connections per data point

Should your enlightenment index be below the minim index as above defined it means you will need to add additional data points to your database to allow enlightenment and a strong data foundation.

The model is supported by the ideology of six degrees of separation.
It is the idea that everyone and everything is connected in 6 degrees or less. This means each of us is a friend of a person that is "friend of a person that is a friend of a person that is a friend of a person that is a friend of Barack Obama". It might be less that people are needed but seldom more.

Data should represent the real world that is why it should follow the same rules.

The concept for first formulated by Stanley Milgram in the 1960s. The idea from an experiment that was testing how much steps it would take to deliver a package from the west coast to a specific person in Boston. The constraint was you can only send it to people you know on a first-name basis. So, each person was sending the package to people that are closer (geographical, from job type or otherwise) to the destination target. What the experiment found out is that it took on average 6 steps to reach the target.

An experiment that was repeated in various ways including the parody of the rule as the six degrees of Kevin Bacon. This was a university experiment of proving that you can connect any actor to Kevin Bacon in 6th via six other actors that starred in a film with each other?

This natural phenomenon is one of the modeling approaches datasets and other world abstractions need to contain to ensure a real-world relevant model.

In the meantime, other studies have shown that six degrees are reducing. Especially due to social media. In 2011 Facebook 72 million users were connected via friendship connections. In an analysis, it showed that 92% of all users were connected via 4 degrees and 99.6% via 5 degrees to each other person in the network. An amazing idea considering that Facebook contains both the most famous actors like Brad Pitt as well as a street shop merchant in middle Europe. And you are probably connected in less than 6 steps to each of them. Suddenly famous does not look that far anymore.

The idea that the number of degrees is shrinking is still in discussion. But a key point to be considered is the strength of connections.

Most people's friend group on Facebook does not represent their real friend group but rather loose acquaintances. This created the idea around strong and weak links that are influencing the number of degrees of separation.

Via strong links you can reach everyone via 6 degrees

Via weak links, you can reach everyone via 4 degrees.

In enlightened data, we are looking for strong connections and each data point needs to be able to be connected data point within a maximum of 6 other data points. Should you reach that level it means you have around a level of data enlightenment that will enable you to connect the dots, that optimal contextualized decisions and ensure option data availability.

Start evaluating enlightened data & spherical databases. Measure the spheres' density & enlightenment index to evaluate how well your dataset is contextualized.

The expiry date of data

Have you ever heard a statement like this?
"There are 2.5 quintillion bytes of data created each day at our current pace, but that pace is only accelerating with the growth of the Internet of Things. Over the last two years alone 90 percent of the data in the world was generated."

What is being ignored is that probably around 80% of that data is outdated by the time anyone records it. Companies today still see that permanently storing data is the right way of approaching their data tactics. Many business IT systems were largely finance systems or ERP or production systems. Most of these systems generated data even if not on a massive scale but they needed to store the information for long term reporting or legal purposes like taxes or fraud prevention. Fast forward 20 years finance systems and ERP systems are largely still existing (and in the case of SAP even large unchanged yet successful) but they do not make up the larger volume of company relevant data. Today's data is largely dark data coming from multiple sources and is numerous is appearance and occurrence but largely uncontrolled and without context.
With GDPR in the year 2016 a first attempt was done by companies to introduce a couple of data reduction guidelines, but mostly only implemented for personal/people-related data. Yet it was a great pointer in the right direction that with items like the "right to be forgotten".
Any dataset should have a "mission impossible like" self-destruction mechanism (or in a less Hollywood version and destruction governance). Many companies have not yet realized that the large amount of data they have about past behaviors has been made obsolete by corona.

This only becomes more evident when we elevate data into information.

The expiry date of the information

- Milk is healthy
- Vitamin C is good for your body
- Germany a World Soccer Champion
- A barrel of oil dropped to 20 dollars per barrel
- My pin codes

You receive thousands of information and facts every day. Your brain is a wonder in how to store massive amounts of information. Images of your childhood. Remembering your friends.

In this book, I talk about the amazing feats your brain accomplishes every minute and every second and why so many technologies emulate your brain to come to a higher level of possibilities. But let me start with something our brains fail to do. We do not have an expiry date for information/knowledge. When have you last time sense checked the learnings you received as a kid? Milk is good, vitamin c is good. The latest studies have proven the opposite.

If you are older you might remember there were studies proving smoking is healthy for your body. Recently you might remember that VW cars received great environmental ratings a few years back. Outdated information by far.

Our brain replaces facts only if a new fact is being brought to us. If there are no new facts, we assume it is still valid. This means that if we do not actively look to update our knowledge and believe our brain assumes the validity of all information.

Every information you receive, and every information has an expiry date.

The same way your milk will get spoilt after some time and your fruits will spoil, so will information. Sometimes to the point of toxicity.

This misbelieve is causing on a personal level illness, obesity, and death; in the business sector wrong decisions, wasted money, and bankruptcy.

One should never take decisions based on outdated information. Facts change over time and your acknowledgment of them needs to change as well.

As a personal exercise, always be cautious when you look to make decisions based on facts that you have known for years. Every time you find yourself in this situation do quick research to see if this is still valid and is this the objective truth.

Our world is accelerating, and every piece of information has a different expiry date, some have days, some years but all of them have one. And all of them are getting smaller and smaller each year.

At work next time you see a slide deck ask your team what are the underlying facts and if the facts have recently been validated?

10 years ago, the concept of open offices was getting traction and see as a path toward cultural transformation and efficiency. 5 years ago, almost all of this was invalidated by dozens of studies and real-world evidence. Yet today there is still a massive amount of companies that are actively pursuing this road not even looking for the latest studies that have proven the opposite. Even after knowing that especially the negative impacts in a social distancing time are enormous.

(Check List) Data as an Asset

- ☐ Data tactics are derived from the business strategy
- ☐ Data tactics should describe how data will be used as a strategic asset but as part of a more data-driven business model
- ☐ Data tactics need to have two sides: Defence vs Attack. Data tactics need to contain the governance, the storage the access, security, and protection as well as strategy to leverage the data for decision making, sharing, and monetizing data.
- ☐ Data tactics is an infinite problem you need to be pragmatic and creative. Knowing that you will never succeed at fully managing data
- ☐ Data tactics need to first design the accessibility of information
- ☐ Data tactics contain three information strategies: Insights to inform business decisions, product development and transactional support
- ☐ Data tactics need to focus on strong automation
- ☐ Rethink completely all your systems landscape
- ☐ 33% of all your effort needs to be on data culture
- ☐ Data tactics need to break silos
- ☐ What are your data ethics?
- ☐ How do you have to expire of data & information
- ☐ Even the absence of data is data

(Tactic) Game theory

If you know the enemy and know yourself, you need not fear the result of a hundred battles. If you know yourself but not the enemy, for every victory gained you will also suffer a defeat. If you know neither the enemy nor yourself, you will succumb in every battle. - Sun Tzu

---

When making decisions a supporting element of decision making is game theory. You probably heard about and you might have seen the movie "a beautiful mind" in which Russell Crow played young mathematicians called Nash. In the movie & real life, John Nash invented the Nash equilibrium and brought game theory to a new level.

Game theory is an arm of decision making that handles specifically decision making when more than one player comes into play. Only because it is called a game it might give you the impression that this is not relevant for business or your day to day interaction. The opposite is true as Game theory largely explains social dynamics and business decision-making strategies.

In this context, a game is defined as any interaction between multiple people in which each person's payoff is affected by decisions made by others.

In principle, there are two main categories of game theory that apply to business: Competitive and Collaborative games. In competitive games game theory helps you how to win & explain decision making done by others. In collaborative games, it helps you to be fair. The key point is always to understand whether the setting of a problem and how you approach a certain problem is generating a competitive or collaborative system.

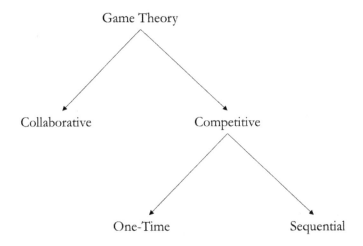

Let us look at competitive systems first.

In most companies, you have yearly performance management including 360 feedback in which employees are providing positive or negative feedback about each other via the manger. Companies usually have a fixed bonus system meaning you might have fix scope of 1.000.000 euro in bonus that will at the end be distributed between employees according to their performance ranking.

During the 360 reviews, the manager talks to for example two employees to receive feedback about each other. The employees now each have the choice to give good feedback or bad feedback about each other. Let us look from the side of the theory.

- If employee 1 give positive feedback about employee 2 and vice versa - both will get a 5k euro bonus
- If employee 1 gives negative feedback about employee 2 and vice versa - both will get a 3k bonus
- If employee 1 gives positive feedback about employee 2 and employee 2 gives negative feedback about employee 1 - the former will get 2k and the later 8k as they will in relative scale to each other look better.

- If employee 1 gives negative feedback about employee 2 and employee 2 gives positive feedback about employee 1 - the former will get 8k and the later 2k as they will in relative scale to each other look better.

	Employee 2 gives positive feedback	Employee 2 gives negative feedback
Employee 1 gives positive feedback	5k/5k	2k/8k
Employee 1 gives negative feedback	8k/2k	3k/3k

What is the best solution for this situation? Unfortunately, the same that is often seen. The best scenario for any employee is to talk negatively about your other employees. It is called a dominant strategy, as independent of what the other employee does, you are better off.

If employee 2 gives positive feedback and you give negative - you gain 8k instead of the 5k.

If employee 2 gives you negative feedback and you give also negative feedback you will gain 3k instead of the 2k.

Have you ever wondered why there is so much negative feedback provided in 360 reviews? Not only is there a psychological pattern behind but there is even from a company standpoint not logical incentive to choose the high road.

Now obviously not everyone follows this pattern, but one key principle is that in many competitive settings if you act outside of your self-interest you only reinforce the self-interest of others.

Does it mean we need a different group of employees? It probably will not help.

You might know the story of circus elephants. Have you ever wondered why such large and majestic beings are usually just controlled by a small rope? Any normal logic will dictate that if an elephant wants to go somewhere else this small rope would never stop them. Yet it did because the elephant got from an environmental side indoctrinated that they can never escape the rope. As a small child, the elephants spent all their time attached to this rope. While they were young the rope was blocking them and no matter how much they pulled they could not escape. Growing with that belief even once they were 10 times the size and no ropes whatsoever could hold them; they still believed this tiny rope is an unmovable obstacle.

When we build systems where the game theory tells us that acting fair and collaborative is not the most effective then we will create a culture of narcissists and complainers (other types of negative traits).

We can use game theory to test if the logic will tell the use of the environment. Our players in this case employees are moving them towards the most optimal outcome. It does not guarantee the right outcome as humans are not always acting rationally but the opposite will always lead to a negative outcome.

Competitive Game Theory

There is also the example of the Tabaco industry. In 1971 the US government banned cigarette advertisements from tv. A few years later all the top Tabaco companies made record profit. A great time for all the shareholders of the tobacco industry. So how come that preventing ads in tv improved the profit for most companies. If we approach it from a game theory angle, then this picture is a lot more logical.

Today all companies were investing in advertisement, and each made around 50m Euro. If they would not have invested in advertisement other players would have stolen their market share. Yet what happened was that the government forced the hand of the big Tabaco in their favor as suddenly they did not have to spend money on advertisement without loss of market share.

	Company 1 does not invest in ads	Company 1 does invest in ads
Company 2 does invest in ads	50/50	80/20
Company 2 does not invest in ads	20/80	75/75

The third element around competitive game theory is iterative games.

In most business challenges we are not in a situation where we only act hidden. Take the example of fuel station pricing. For most industries price setting is public and thus can be not following under the hidden decision matrix we had before, but the visible and iterative meaning you can take action after you or the other competition took an action.

Let us look again at the matrix we had above for two fuel stations that are next to each other on two sides of the street.

In their street, every day 100 people are fueling their cars. If they have the same price point the split is largely 50/50. If one has a lower price point, they will get a larger share of 70/30. If both are having their price point, they will have still a 50/50 split but at a lower price leading to 40 / 40 in the outcome.

To make it easier we assume the starting price on that day is 1 Euro & as many cars come in the morning as in the afternoon.

Before noon:

	A Keeps price at the same level	A Decreases Prices to 10%
B Keeps price at the same level	50/50	63/30
B Decreases Prices 10%	30/63	45/45

Before noon if fuels station a) has decreased price:

	A Keeps price at the same level	A Decreases Prices 10%
B Keeps price at the same level	63/30	70/15
B Decreases Prices 10%	45/45	57/27

Following the theory, we would reach a point whereby lowering your price would be better off. Yet in an iterative game like this, the competition can adjust and would also reduce their price. Which would create a new game theory situation, which would after applying the same theory would lead to a downward cycle price reduction. Great for customers and bad for the company.

In iterative game theory, there are two rules we can derive.
a) If you are the first actor - you always should choose the option that creates the highest value for both candidates.
b) if you are the second actor you should always cooperate with the first to ensure maximum pay-out.

If you extend this to 3 options which include increase, decrease, and hold the price this becomes even more obvious.

Game theory is not just applying to 2 by 2 matrix or 3 x 3 but can easily be scaled to 10 by 10 or 30 by 30 matrix. By using search for dominant strategies and eliminating lower options even large-scale decision matrix can be broken down into the best solution path. One by one we will be looking for one strategy that will be more effective than another and removing the line/column from the matrix.

We have two competitors of chocolate bars trying to sell their products. Today they have a 50 / 50 market and combined sales of 10 m euro.
They have a certain budget to choose to invest in one of the channels Advertisement, Sales Rebates, social media, Customer Influencer, Events, Sponsoring. Each channel has a different pay-out and impact either getting new customers that did not buy chocolate or customers of the competition.

A/B Marketshare	A				
	Ads	Sales Rebates	Social media	Customer Influencer	Sponsoring
Ads	50/50	60/40	55/45	60/40	33/66
Sales Rebates	40/60	50/50	40/60	45/55	25/75
Social media	45/55	60/40	50/50	45/55	33/66
Customer Influencer	40/60	55/45	55/45	50/50	25/75
Sponsoring	66/33	75/25	66/33	75/25	50/50

When you analyze this matrix in which channel would you invest?

If you look for a dominant strategy you will choose sales rebates. Yet this would only be a one-level strategy. In the next step, other companies need to adjust. Over time both companies will reach the same price but will have destroyed market value.

If you look for a sustainable strategy it would be that you choose **social media** as investments. Why? No matter what strategy player B chooses choosing social media or customer influencers is more effective than ads or sponsoring thus eliminating these options.

This leads to the below matrix

		A	
A/B Marketshare		Social media	Customer Influencer
	Ads	55/45	60/40
	Sales Rebates	40/60	45/55
B	Social media	50/50	45/55
	Customer Influencer	55/45	50/50
	Sponsoring	66/33	75/25

Company B is also not stupid and will not choose to invest primarily in sponsoring or Ads. Leading to the below matrix:

		A	
A/B Marketshare		Social media	Customer Influencer
	Sales Rebates	40/60	45/55
B	Social media	50/50	45/55
	Customer Influencer	55/45	50/50

Seeing this you would in 2 out of 3 cases in social media get a better result than if you would go for customer influencers.
Only if the other company goes for market destruction like the rebates you would lose out, but it can be adjusted after rather quickly.

Collaborative Game theory

Whereas competitive game theory is teaching how to win. Collaborative game theory is about being fair. It largely helps us to define the value of individual players and share rewards in the most optimal way.

Let us take the shoe companies Adidas and Puma.
In 2018 Puma had a revenue of 4.64 billion euros and Adidas 21.9 billion euro. If over time the two realize that they largely eat each other's market share rather than attacking the 36,39 billion market that Nike is controlling. In this fictive scenario, the two realize that if they co-operate that they could increase their combined revenue from 26.5 to 33 billion by refocusing their marketing strategy & supporting each other. So how would we determine the value of each company in this collaboration?
Game Theory provides here a few rules in connection to the "Shapley value", which is a method of splitting gains/costs among players according to their value linked to their contributions:

a) The contribution of each player is determined by what is lost by removing them from the equation. This is called the marginal contribution. In our case this means that the value of Adidas is determined as the value of the coalition (33 billion) - the value of the coalition without them, which in this case it would just Puma and they would drop back to their original sales of 4.64 billion = 33 - 4.64 = Value of Adidas 28.36 billion. The value of Puma is 33 - 21.9 = 11.1 billion.

b) Interchangeable players have the same value. If in our case, we could exchange Puma with New Balance in our coalition then they both would have the same value. In another setting, it also means that employees that do the same work at the same speed/proficiency and quality should get the same pay.
c) Dummy players have zero value. If we would add a player that does not contribute anything, they should not be entitled to get anything in return. Of course, in business management generosity, helpfulness, and supporting others should always be considered.
d) If a process has multiple parts costs & value should be decomposed across those parts. If puma and Adidas would have split their agreement into separate parts of the supply chain e.g. Production and Marketing/Selling, then the value function needs to be the sum of both value change parts.

Meaning that the revenue split is only part of the equation but it could be that Puma is significantly better at the production and overall cost management and their marginal contribution towards the coalition in this area far outweighs their value in marketing and selling thus raising their overall contribution of what we calculated before.

How to apply this to project bonus payments

In general, I was always a supporter of project-based bonus payments with milestone-based agreements rather than individual bonus payments on combined year performance. Over time I saw many of the team members getting excited about these project awards leading to better results not only because of the financials but also via them there was a concrete target of what to archive and a clear correlation between project results & reward.

The tough part was around splitting the reward fairly between the individual team members. In this case, we had 1 Junior

Data Scientist, 2 Senior Data Scientist, 1 Project Manager, 1 Change Manager, and 1 Analytics Business translator. Each person worked full-time on the project but not everyone had the same impact. The junior data scientist only delivered 30% of the scope that the Senior Data Scientist got. Should he/she still get the same bonus as the other team members? Knowing that I will never be able to be fair, at least I can build a model that I can explain and justify. I approached it with the following thinking:

1) The value of the project was 10m Euro with an investment of 100k creating an ROI of 100.
2) Senior Data Scientist 1 and Senior Data Scientist 2 were having the same productivity, behavior, skills, and influence in the project and should get the same value (Interchangeability of players)
3) The project went through different phases, and I assigned the value of each person during each phase resulting in the below. The value was defined as if I remove them from the equation(the project) what is the impact of timelines, cost, quality, impact translated into ROI.
The project runs through the phases of Initiation (Design, Governance, Project setup), Implementation/Insight Phase(Requirements details, Coding, Analytics, testing), and Insight to Impact phase(Training, Convincing, ensuring management understands the results and turn the results into actions).

If I remove the project manager, we would have still delivered the project probably at the same quality but with missing coordination & missing people engagement, we would have delivered 20% slower & wasted 20% of the cost in each phase. The PM was more impactful than expected as his engaging nature accelerated other's works and increased their motivation.

If I remove one of the senior data scientists, the cost during the implementation phase would be 50% slower and during the impact phase 10% less due to some experts not being able to join meetings needed to explain the technical aspect of the project.

If I remove the Change manager, the impact phase will be impacted as we would not have the right access to management, not the right training, not the right ambassadors and it will impact based on our experience the impact phase by 60%.

If I remove the translator, we will see a 30% impact in the quality of the design, 10% due to missing clarity in the implementation, and 40% during the impact phase due to missing translation from insight to action to impact.

This led to the following:

The total impact of each person on the total project was 370 points as I considered all three phases being equally important. As a result, I was then looking at the 25k bonus for the team and was splitting it according to the individual's marginal contribution we came to the following results:

- Junior = 30 / 370 * 25k = 2.0k
- Senior = 70 / 370 * 25k = 4.7k
- Senior =70 / 370 * 25k = 4.7k
- PM =60 / 370 * 25k = 4.1k
- CM = 60 / 370 * 25k = 4.1k
- Translator = 80 / 370 * 25k = 5.4k

Probably not everyone agrees with that approach, but it helped me structure my thoughts. It eliminated the problem that more visible people than others received higher recognition & bonus pay-outs in past projects due to personal biases me & others had. Approaching it this way also helped me in later discussions about the team member's performance to explain their numbers as well as their improvement points.

How do game theory and data science work together?

Game Theory is impacting your data science on what solutions you can build but also on how you need to behave in the future. Most projects that I have seen in analytics are looking at the market in a rather singular fashion. If I invest in more marketing my sales increase will become 15% higher. Analytics like "investment effectiveness", "marketing mix/channel mix analytics" or "customer segmentation" is a great start in redefining what marketing is best for you and how you should act to improve sales. But all of them assume that the competition is either too stupid to notice, too preoccupied, or too slow. If you enrich the above models with the game theory about projecting cooperation or competition games and which moves the other market player will do in relation to your moves, you can truly change the game.

I project that soon companies that have the right decision-making AI based on data science & game theory will dominate the marketplace. There will be a race in each industry towards a game theory data science AI on business strategy with the first major impacts by the latest 2023.

Secondly the more we automate and the more we do the "logical" decisions the more predictable as a company will we become. AI systems are monitoring your moves and each of your partners & competition will collect data about your interactions/reaction with them. They will use AI to analyze what is the best strategy to gain more than they gain today. We will need to learn that while our idea is to be logical in many cases it will pay to do the counter-intuitive. Within the game theory, it is called a mixed strategy. It does not mean that we should spread fake information or that we should flip a coin, but that sometimes taking a riskier bet that might not be the most logical choice will gain in value as a competition AI will not assume this as the logical action for you. Mix your logical strategies with surprises for your competition.

If a basketball player is great at dunking, he will dunk all the time and it will make him predictable and easier defendable leading to him scoring less. By adding a few 3-point long-range shots it will allow a higher and less easily protectable result.

Use game theory to test your people & partnership models Use game theory to find the best

Do things counter-intuitive – balance competitive game theory and a mixed strategy

---

(Tactic) Be where others are not

It is simple. If you play the same strategy as the market leader you will never surpass the market leader. It is due to the economy of scale of learning. If you try a lot of things, you learn a lot more than if you would do less. The only way how to overcome a market leader is to look for where they are not. You need to know your strength but also the others' weakness. If the market leader is strong at attracting older generations try focusing on the younger first. If the leader is strong at a certain feature, try not to be better in that feature find another feature where you can make the difference. Do not try to be a copycat product.

When strong, avoid them. If of high morale, depress them. Seem humble to fill them with conceit. If at ease, exhaust them. If united, separate them. Attack their weaknesses. Emerge to their surprise. – Sun Tzu

---

(Tactic) Where focus goes energy flows

One tactic is to focus on energy. Which means resources, people, financials, and most importantly attention. Two key variants have shown success in the past. Extreme focus and rotating focus.

Extreme focus is when you concentrate solely on one topic. Take Apple as an example once again. Steve Jobs when he came back to apple looked at all the great things that were going on. Multiple different computer models, software applications, and addon devices, yet the company were in a deep struggle to manage. Luckily, Microsoft was investing in Apple at this point and Steve Jobs was taking over. Microsoft invested in Apple to a large extent to ensure there is not the perception of a monopoly which usually would lead to a breakup of the market or company.
Steve with a certain level of financial backing decided to go to extreme focus. He mentioned that when asked by a family member which Apple PC should she buy, that he was not able to answer this at all. If he cannot choose, how can a consumer choose? Thus, he reduced all computers to one model. Only one model. He stopped all software and addons. To focus on solely 1 computer. This led to a complete upward trend that allowed the company to strife. Apple did not stay with just one product long after, but here is where there is an easy guideline:

If you are unsuccessful focus to an extreme.

If you are on a successful wave, diversify and try to be on the next wave.

Rotating focus is used in marketing by the mid-size player with a much lower investment capacity vs e.g. the market leader. In most industries and markets marketing is driven by your financial constraints. Companies invest in TV ads, social advertisements, influencers, sales reps, and sales events. Yet usually for a smaller player it is impossible to even invest in one channel as much as the market leader. Some companies decided that creating a rotating focus to overcome this market disparity. Based on psychology it is known that people only remember the very highs and the very lows, this is what rotating focus among other advantages tackles.

The idea is basically that you invest in each month everything into a single channel. The next month you invest in another channel.

- In January you focus everything on sales reps visiting customers
- In February all the sales reps and resources get focused on email marketing
- In March you focus on web events or TV ads.
- You repeat each quarter

If you cannot be the best in everything all the time, you still can be the best at everything at a given time.

(Tactic) Digital ethics, Digital Security, and New Risks

Digital unfortunately does not only offer opportunities it does pose new types of ethical dilemmas and security risks.

Last year at a conference in Berlin on stage I was asked what we can do about making sure that our technology is ethical and compliant. We had just talked about the negative impact of robotics, killer drones (literally), and deep fakes.

The simple answer was: "Be human".

We control technology. We design if the technology is doing the right or wrong thing. There is no unethical AI. There is no unethical digital solution. There are no discriminating algorithms.

There are only unethical developers and data that is based on discriminating behaviors. There is only unethical data that represents unethical human behavior today.

Most of us do not even understand the full breadth of the internet. We only access the clear web, thus what we can access via google or other search engines. Both the deep web as well as the dark web are widely unknown to the public. Estimates say the size of the deep web at between 96% and 99% of the internet.

The Deep Web is all the sites on the web that cannot be reached with a search engine. This contains your intranet (can't be accessed via google) but many other platforms.

The Darknet, is a collection of websites on an encrypted network with hidden IP addresses, leading to strong anonymity protection.

The usage of data also brings new challenges. What are the symptoms of a heart attack?

Did you think about **Dizziness, Heartburn, Cold sweat, Tiredness, Nausea?**

No? There is a high chance that what you just thought about are the MALE symptoms of a heart attack. Women suffer more heart attacks than men but with different symptoms especially below 45. Depending on the study up to 50% of female heart attacks are misdiagnosed as panic attacks and wrong treatment is provided.

This alone is disappointing. Imagine you build a diagnosis AI on this. If you simply use the past you will enhance the disparity between gender-based diagnosis.

With a group of friends, we were helping a few investment start-ups for their AI development. In one start-up we lived through how unethical decisions can happen if we are not careful. One AI that was build was proposing to invest in a certain cosmetics company. The return per employee was extraordinary. Only when we went deeper into understanding why the model would propose this, we realized that the model found out that the company has a massive amount of female sales reps. In the first moment, we thought maybe because the customers of the products are largely female that a female sales rep in combination with the female customers were a good fit. It took two more levels of analyzing the AI to figure out: The company has mostly female sales reps as they could pay them 33% less than males sales reps driving up profit way above the industry norm. Of course, the AI was not unethical, the underlying company was and probably no human investor would have caught that driver, but you do not want to endorse this way of acting. You have a new level of accountability. Like the great philosopher spiderman said:

"With great power comes great responsibility."

A few days ago, I was in a company conference call. While the topic was not the most confidential it was still an important topic. In the middle of the conference, my watch starts reacting. In the sweet voice of Siri telling me: "Sorry I did not catch that". While the whole conference was laughing at a rather comical situation at that moment, I also realized that literally, we had another company listening to every strategic discussion. Even saying hello from time to time.

Data privacy. Data confidentiality. A permanent connection to the internet and loss of control is something you will need to address.

Despite all that ethics & compliance are also an opportunity. Transparency means you have a more equal playing field. Ethics can become a differentiating factor in your value proposition.

Think about how you use ethics and compliance to your advantage as much as reducing risk.

(Tactic) No-touch Low-touch

One of the greatest experiences any manager will have is to (for a while) join a start-up to learn their way of working. It will open your eyes to what is possible. Ironically even more in backend processes than on their products themselves. Over years companies have outsourced work to cheap labor countries. Go to any of these companies and ask them if it will be possible to insource this or to automate what is done by the outsourcing partner and you will get a clear NO. Then go to a start-up or company that only exists for 5 years. You will realize that they are not considering outsourcing because simply the big complex process steps are not existing. Millions in revenue are managed by 1 accountant will a few only applications. Electronic invoicing is the norm. Contracts are sent and orders confirmed via WhatsApp. If you are later joining a game, you often have the advantage of bypassing a lot of the complexity. China as a country has almost completely bypassed email and went directly to WeChat (messenger). Imagine this in your company.
Nevertheless, you can change this, but it requires rethinking how you approach processes. To redesign processes, you need to raise one question to you.
How would this process work if no one would have to touch it or only 2 times a process can be touched. Sometimes you will see it will require automation, sometimes it means that you stop certain parts of processes, sometimes it means that we will need to adjust the input is done, sometimes it might be AI, sometimes it might be integrating into online services. If you look at how to automate a process you already are in the wrong question. We need to fundamentally redesign your process to gain value.

How can you get inspired? Go to google and search:
"Accounting systems for start-ups"
"Human Resource management for start-ups"

Look at the solutions and steal the design ideas to inspire your way of working and your tools.

Suddenly we might just realize that the only blocker to transform our process is us and our framed thinking.

(Tactic) Digital identity

In recent months I had quite a lot of discussions at conferences and with other companies around digital. One topic I refer to in these discussions is the "Digital Identity" in a company. The name might be different from one company to another, including variations like Digital Fitness or Digital Psychology, but every company has these types of discussions in one way or another.

In short "Digital Identity" is the aggregation of all employee mindsets and all competencies to embrace, understand, and effectively use digital ways of working to create superior value. Every company I talked to is agreeing that what distinguishes great digital transformations from unsuccessful transformations is people and their mindset – never just technology.

Every digital transformation without
human transformation is bound for failure

It is often more about accepting that the world is digital and that not participating in the digital world is not an option. If the past has not shown this, then corona has proven it.

Digital is around thinking in a digital world. Your customer, your team members, your car even your fridge is digitally connected. We WhatsApp, we Snap, we Twitter, we Google. Nothing proves world domination more than when a company name becomes an officially approved verb.

Digital is about how you change your company but also how to understand the ecosystem around. It is as much about knowing how AI can be used to generate customer value as much as knowing how to use TikTok to influence your customers.

While processes and of course technology play their role, they are not ensuring progressive value generation on the same level as the right people do. Yet while there is agreement on this point, the answer on "what kind of profiles are needed" often ends with blanks or with generalized statements like "data scientists" or "cool nerds".

Before I go into what Digital Identity means I would like to cover one very common question: "Do we need everyone to become digital leaders in the next 3 years".

The clear answer is: No. But I believe there is a large portion of any company that needs to evolve towards a greater digital identity to ensure growth to not be left behind.

What I believe in, is a company digital transformation at three digital gears. The first gear consists of people who grow towards an evolved digital identity with a high focus on high-value projects/discussions/partnering/innovation which can or should lead to multiple companies elevating disruptions(technology or none technology-based). Using digital ways of working and open-minded approaches this part of finance drives major changes in the organization.

The second gear is the part of the organization that uses its digital identity towards "quick wins" or "continuous improvements" and makes the best out of our existing processes. They rely for the most part on current skills injected with a growing amount of digital skills.

The third gear is foundational groups which include the larger set of operations (e.g. run the day to day transactions) where the growth of the digital identity is not at the forefront of people's development plans in the next years.

Important is the mix between the three groups in the next years. I believe we will need to move towards a 30/40/30 distribution of these groups in the next years. The numbers are mostly driven by the need to have a critical mass to create sustainable analysis and the critical mass to drive decisions based on digital models while balancing the day to day activities. This means that soon I believe we will require to focus on building digital leaders for the first and second gear thus shifting the digital talents/hires to the right positions.

Let us now look at the idea of what a digital identity consists of. First, as for every other identity, the visible parts are "Mindset" and "Competencies". In other words, your Digital Identity is defined as the sum of your Digital Mindset Value and Digital Competencies, with each being split into the following subcategories.

- Digital Mindset
    - Value generation focus instead of efficiency-focused
    - Disruption (incl. innovation) instead of Continuous Improvement
    - Speed instead of perfection
    - Trust instead of control
    - Creation mindset instead of Consumer mindset
    - Do not think outside the box, think there is no box

- Digital Competencies
    - Adaptive high-speed learning
    - Creative problem solving instead of adopting best practice
    - Influencing and driving change in an imperfect information environment

Value generation focus instead of efficiency-focused:
The mindset of successful digital leaders is for the majority of
items focused on how to increase the generated value and how
to help to create new value areas from scratch rather than
focusing on improving how we can reduce the effort in what
we are doing today. While this encapsulates more risks than a
more traditional approach the reward for the company as well
as the individual is much higher leading to sustainable retention
and success. The foundation required of this not to fear failure.
From a management side, this requires us to encourage new
value generation approaches, next to efficiency focus, and
giving a real room for failing fast to your team members. While
many say "it is fine to fail" in most leadership teams the
communication style and actions do not represent their verbal
openness(e.g. An employee fails and their name is being used
as a negative example for months).

Disruption Instead of Continuous Improvement
Continuous improvement has been a major milestone in how
to ensure progress, but it also led to a lowering of ambition
level. By constantly looking for quick wins, we often lose the
big picture possibilities. If you only look at your feet while
walking you will not end up where you wanted to. While quick
gains are helpful to increase credibility, they are likely not
breaking the glass ceiling of sustainable performance.
Otherwise, you might look back 3 years from now and feel like
we moved a lot but progressed little. As a management team
we have to be careful to avoid phrases like: "We did not
manage to do this in the past", "I do not believe it is possible"
and if it should not work out, do not come with the "I could
have told you it will not work".
If our team members believe they have an approach, let them
do it. I can guarantee you that in most cases where a person
can visualize a solution, they can make it real. As Steve Jobs
quote:

Because people who are crazy enough to think they can change the world, actually do - Steve Jobs

---

Speed instead of perfection

One of the most frustrating experiences in the digital world is the fight for having perfect data and perfect results, especially in an imperfect information world. While we should push for the best possible data, looking for 100% perfection is the death of progress and the death of impact. By the time you reach 100% the world has turned, and new problems occurred setting you back to 0%. The world is turning at a higher speed than ever before and reacting to it is increasingly difficult while ensuring perfection. While challenging results to make them good, also reflect as of which moment we are just a challenge for the sake of challenging. Taking a perfect decision too late is also not perfect.

Trust instead of control

I am here talking about trust towards people and not the trust in technology. Projects in a digital setup like advanced analytics are extremely complex and fast-changing in an ambiguous world. Contrary to many other technical projects, they are unpredictable in terms of outcome and require us to pivot heavily. But instead of over-controlling individual people, we need to trust those that dedicate days of work in looking for approaches to create maximum impact. As a management team rather than involving our self in every decision (+Which causes dozen of people discussing and changing decision(without new information available regularly) we need to put the right people/team together on the right projects/streams and will trust that they will do right things (with as little outside steering as possible).

BUT right people are based on capabilities and mindset, not only because of "they have availabilities" or because "it is their job/hierarchy level".

Creation mindset instead of Consumer mindset

If I would have to choose the biggest differentiator in digital mindset vs a non-digital mindset it would be this.

In the non-digital mindset even in projects where people are the leader, they are mostly looking at "consuming" technologies that will be implemented in the project. They look at "experts" to tell them what the limits are and how others are using them. The same is true for many leads who expect others to pre-think creational elements for them by others. Each member of a digital project is an Intrapreneur (Entrepreneur within a company).

Whenever you ask, "Can analytics do this" or "When will others tell me what to do next", you are raising the wrong questions. A digital leader is curious in any way to find a way where there seems to be none. In the digital mindset, you are looking and proactively proposing how to create the most valuable solution – even without any technical skills.

The questions should be: "How can I use analytics and other items to solve this problem."

As a management team, I would ask everyone to encourage intrapreneurship within your team members.

Adaptive high-speed learning.

Talking here about my personal experience. A few weeks back I looked at my skills(digital/technical) developed in the last 12 years.

A shocking revelation was that almost 90% of what I learned 10 years ago is completely irrelevant today. Not just in my job, but even if I would be in the same position. Even worse 80% of the skills I had 5 years ago are irrelevant now. And most depressing over 30% of my skills learned last year are already irrelevant. Instead in the digital world, it is constant learning of what is new, what is possible, and what more I can do, that is a critical asset.

Learning how to learn, is a skill. After a summit, a couple of participants came to me and said: "I believe digital is important, but I am not sure I can learn it. I stopped learning 10 years ago and this is just too new." As a management team, I believe we need to support our team members how they can learn new things every few weeks, be it through coaching, formal training, or self-learning.

Every learning needs to be born out of positivity does not fear.

Creative problem solving instead of best practice:

Google, Amazon, SAP, IBM, start-ups, etc, publish new algorithms, products, and services every few hours and a new post about new approaches that have been invented every time you refresh your browser. Most "best practices" are obsolete by the time they are written down. While they might contain learnings we should consider, the most important is to approach every problem from the right angle. Which potential technologies, approaches, best practice solve the problems in the best way in our existing situation with the exact amount of people and the exact circumstances involved. Taking many diverse skills and knowledge to solve problems best. As a management team, I would look at still to encourage "outside-in" but let us not understate our capabilities to solve problems.

Influencing and driving change in an imperfect environment:

Even the greatest analytics is not a success if it does not lead to action or behavior changes. Unfortunately, this requires often very uncomfortable discussions. The world is not perfect and expecting perfect analysis from your team members is thus unrealistic. We often do the unrealistic comparison of expecting 10x as much accuracy/details from our analysts than from fellow humans. Looking at some of the discussions we had in the last 4 weeks we got feedback like: "I believe a 50%

accurate prediction with false arguments more than a statistically 90% accurate number without arguments." Do not forget statistics are arguments as well, we are just not used to understand their language. So rather than asking analytics to provide the arguments in the same form we used in the past, we need to look for how we can use the arguments of analytics to incorporate them into our storytelling.

Do not think outside the box, think there is no box:

Some think inside the box, those that think outside the box, and those that think there is no box. When you limit your mind, you create boundaries that you could overcome otherwise. If you think your "Silos" is an obstacle you will look for a solution within the silos and not how to break them, thus limiting your ultimate value proposition. If your solution provides such a substantial value no one would challenge it if the solution came from outside the box or was created without considering the "box".

(Tactic) Recruitment Revolution

Hoping that you have all the right people in your company is great and if you do then it is amazing. In most cases, companies are not so lucky and need to bring in outside expertise.
A problem when recruiting is that for a large part, we are looking for the wrong signals.
If someone has a gap in their CV - who cares.
Where did they work 5 years ago and 8 years ago – who cares.
What is their degree? - who cares. In a generation where many took sabbaticals to travel the world and learn new cultures gaps years are the norm. Steve Jobs took classes in calligraphy, in most companies the recruiter would have disqualified him.

Most tech companies have long waved the need to have a degree required for top tech jobs, yet other industries have not yet adopted.

Most of the "genius" level technical CEOs like Bill Gates, Steve Jobs and Woz or Bezos none of them had a degree in IT related something. But when normal companies want to hire, they look experts with 10 years of experience a certain education in a field that only exists for 5 years.

In recruitment it comes down to two things:
- Does their personality fit into your team?
- "How" are they thinking, not what are they thinking

In interviews, I usually go through 7 questions in my interviews, but I ask multiple times "why did you make this choice" or "what did you think to come to that conclusion". This way you can remove the bias you have towards people that just interview great and say a few goods things and to include those that are too nervous in the meeting but take the time to think.

Generally, every interview should keep the other person at the edge of comfort and discomfort. I will try to make them feel safe but keep asking them unique questions or strange follow-ups. This edge of comfort I found the most interesting to find out most about people's thinking in a short amount of time that you have in an interview. And it already starts with the intro. After explaining the position and introducing myself I start with.

"I have read your CV. Tell me something interesting that is not on this CV".

It is a question most are not prepared to answer directly. Most have prepared a 30 min speech about their CV (the longer the answer the more likely they want to avoid detailed questions). Yet we are not looking for a person who is great memorizing or holding speeches.

After that I would go into a job-specific type of questions.

7 questions to ask in a data science/digital interview:

Question 1: What is the biggest problem in data science projects

If they say data, red flag. Anyone who blames the data has not understood the overall project and goal.
Data is an obstacle, not a problem. This answer usually comes from people who only look at their small part of an analytical journey and who value the technical/academic development over the impact/customer value it can generate.

Question 2: Ask them how they would solve a certain problem - give a real case
To test the technical approach as well as learn how they think. The biggest give away for a good data scientist - they ask amazing questions.
It does not matter if they solved the case at the end but if the questions were great you are probably on the right track.

Question 3: Explain an algorithm e.g. random forest/regression / deep learning to a kid (it is usually the same as executive level)

If you have a top-notch analytics team, they will be at the table on most critical company decisions ranging from people's decisions to investment opportunities and operational guidance. You need to explain things at a clarity level that is both simple and effective. Many analysts never had management exposure so asking them how they would explain it to the CFO is usually not easy for them. Asking them to explain it to a child (or even their child) is an exciting way of learning if they understood the algorithm but most importantly if they can adapt their communication(and yes it works if you reuse that answer for management)

Question 4: If you could set up a team: Who and which skills would you like in your team

I use this question for any position from data scientists to product manager to head of department. It is a great way to evaluate if a person can holistically see a project. A red flag is if data scientists cannot come up with other key roles than their own as it is an indicator that they don't understand the overall complexity

Question 5: What project are they the proudest of

Everything we do needs to come from positivity and there is nothing more effective than past proud achievements of oneself.

Do not ask linked to their job necessarily, any achievement is great.

In the end, you have a feeling about what makes a candidate proud on the other hand more importantly you create a positive experience.

Question 6: What are the latest trends in technology for your type of company/ what is the impact of corona on the company you are applying

Many candidates I talked to were proud that they did some research about the workplace. Knowing myself how I would have done it in the past (of taking a few notes and memorizing them), I like to put candidates in a position to contextualize trends or events and their importance for a company that you spend hours research. Use this thinking as an ability to judge their contextualization.

Question 7: How would you answer to a colleague who says your data can't be trusted because it is biased

I use this question to analyze how they think about conflict and assertiveness. Do they go into the defense, do they try to bullshit their way through, and are they smoothly convincing me?

7 skills you are looking for in digital people

Skill 1: Entrepreneurial mindset
Any employee that you want to hire needs to be entrepreneurial at heart. Digital is all about reaching new frontiers and overcoming obstacles. You want the entrepreneurs/intrapreneurs in your corner. Digital is disrupting our thinking and you want the disrupters coming from your team and not the competition

Skill 2: Asking and challenging balanced with listening and trying
A personal key revelation in business was when I realized that I know nothing and that this makes me equal to everyone else. When looking for people I am looking for individuals that listen to everyone around and taking the pieces that are most interesting to then try them on their own. You don't want people who follow other teachings to the letter. You want them to have a challenging mind that enhances their thinking through their ideas and others.
I was raised as always critical to myself and what am I doing. Initially, I considered this a major weakness but soon learned that by dissecting my ideas again and again to challenge myself, I build stronger ideas and concepts and was prepared to challenge others to get to better results.

Skill 3: A person who understands they don't know everything but also that others do neither
I believe I am always wrong. And I believe everyone else is wrong. You are looking for profiles that look at everything around them critically. You don't want people that only trust their ideas, as they will not listen well to others' experiences, But you also don't want people that don't have trust in their thinking, thus constantly challenging only their ideas and too

blindly follow others. Critical thinking means not looking at everything negative but rather understand that truth and perspective are not the same. We need profiles that learn from the experiences of others to amplify their own thinking.

Skill 4: They can focus
There are extreme cases in this one. Going to university with many hardcore programmers I learned a new level of focus. We had some students that at times in class could not concentrate for 10 minutes. Partially because of boredom partially because of lack of interest, partially because of a long night before. I always thought of myself to be more superior in terms of focus and thus in productivity. Until one day we worked on a group assignment. Not the most fun part of the university, but you got to know people a lot better. It was around developing a small game in a group of 4 students. We had 7 days' time and met on the first day to start discussing. We talked for like 15 min about the concept and who does what to then go work on our individual parts. Four hours later I felt exhausted I was developing the whole time straight and needed a break. Only to realize that no one else had yet taken a break. This situation went on for another 8 hours. Till today I believe some never even went to the bathroom. But the extreme focus done by people I believed had no ability to concentrate was truly amazing and produced a wonderful product. To game was amazing, even if we got a bad grade as we misunderstood a large part of the exercise.
Since that day I believe that a team member that can place themself into such a tunnel can truly help you build greatness. They have the focus skill and the motivation they will elevate your digital team to a new level.

Skill 5: They can visualize the future
No one can really see the future, but you can create it. Visualizing the future and how the end state of a product looks like on the first day is a fundamental skill in the digital world. This skill which is largely a type of creative decomposition and

analytical composition is what has made. People like Steve Jobs or Mark Zuckerberg might not be the greatest humans but they were great product visionaries.

In your team today you will have people who have this skill. Look and you will find them, even if in the most hidden parts of your organization.

Skill 6: Open to new technologies but not driven by them
Digital does not mean technology-focused. Most digital people are more focused on the people or business pieces at technology parts. In the famous words of the TV series Startup: "Steve Job could not even code". Digital means that you can use all available technologies interchangeably to reach your goals. Tools, Data, and way of thinking. Having 10 wearables does not make you digital. Thinking how each wearable is can be used to solve your latest business problem, does.

Skill 7: They try - in digital, you can try everything
Experiment, Build, Fail, Repeat, Succeed - end of day 1
Digital is the only area of creation where you can build complete experience in a matter of seconds. Destroy and repurpose all the items with one mouse click. And do this 5 times for 1 day.
Digital means that you try things. Rather than long term evaluating if something is possible and to study what works best, you always will archive greater results by going NIKE: Just DO IT. (And throw away after if not needed)

7 key elements you need to rethink recruitment

To get the right talents you need to act better than those around you. There a few ways on how we need to change recruitment thinking in our companies to reach the goal.

Element 1: The importance of candidate experience speed of recruitment
It's obvious but still, no one cares. At a time where many of your employees are millennials who have learned that within minutes (and a bit of swiping right) you can get a bank account, a social media page, a web business created or get a date, you can not excite people about your company agility by having a three-month application cycle. By using AI and better-designed processes you can create an experience that is a value proposition of your company.
For this:

A) Use AI and every CV that fits the Ai automatically schedule an interview the next day in the second they apply
B) In the second round of interviews have all interviewers lined up behind each other and have the offer prepared. At the end of the interview directly offer or tell the person they are rejected/parked. You already made up your mind anyway. Don't "bench" people for no reason.

Element 2: The importance of employer branding
Invest in your employer branding. More and more you are competing with the same profiles that are looking also at google or amazon. You can get the talents if you build your employer branding. How to best do it? Ask your marketing team. That is their job but just a slightly different target audience

Element 3: The importance of talent pool

I truly believe in the importance of diversity in a department and the company. Nevertheless, many that I talk to are not yet sharing the same enthusiasm. The one argument that convinces most is that by opening your door for diversity

Element 4: The importance of talent pool New recruitment channels like virtual fairs

Use new recruitment channels. While many companies consider LinkedIn to be a novel recruitment channel it is not. Use it as part of your "multichannel" recruitment strategy but also enhance it by have virtual fairs. Many virtual recruitment fairs jumped drastically due to COVID. You meet 100s of talents from all over the world to connect to.

Element 5: Gig Economy

Expect that your internal people will make less and less of your overall workforce. The trend towards a Gig economy with many temporary short-term assignments is growing. Not yet in large companies but it is in small. You are looking for one person to do a code review of your AI system use e.g. "uWork". You have a person doing the job the next day, getting paid and the transaction concluded.

Element 6: Data-driven recruiting and HR Analytics

Selecting CVs for best matches. AI (not fitting profiles will be manually analyzed). Scanning Job descriptions for bias. AI. Personalized messages to applicants. AI. Personalized recruitment invites to people on LinkedIn. AI (if consent is given.
AI will drastically change the way of working in HR. At the last HR conference, I went too I heard the statement that AI tools and digital HR are not yet mature. I believe the

opposite. I believe you already have the tools in your company you just call them marketing tools you just are not targeting them in the needed direction.

Element 7: Social recruiting is much more than just posting ads. Social recruiting is utilizing social media channels such as Facebook, Twitter, LinkedIn, and websites and blogs like Glassdoor to connect to, find, attract, and hire talent. You proactively search for potential candidates, build a relationship with them prior & post recruitment activities, keep with candidates engaged throughout the process as well as afterward, and encourage them to apply for your vacant job positions.

7 Roles of the future

Below you will find 7 roles that I believe will raise in the next 5 years.

Role 1: Lead data (flow) orchestrator
Realizing that data can't be managed in the way we are doing today you need more orchestrators that design the flow and make sure your data is reaching the right place at the right time. They are guiding the river of data in the right direction.

Role 2: Intelligent Automation, process redesign & robotics lead
You will need people that combine the ability to redesign process in a way that maximizes the value of AI systems, RPA, automation technology as well as human input. They will design solutions in a way that each process step creates a secondary value output.

Role 3 AI & Decision-making psychologist
Taking the right actions at the right time will combine specialists that use psychology, game theory, and AI.

Role 4: Competition & customer psychologists
If the former is about how you can take decision in the best way, this role is about understanding why competition does certain actions or why consumers buy products a vs b.

Role 5: Digital partnership lead
80% of all digital solutions your company uses will not be built by you. Therefore, you will need experts in partnering with other companies in a much faster and more speedy way than today.

Role 6: Digital Coach
Different levels of maturity in digital can become a nightmare to manage for companies. You will start hiring coaches that continuously teach and coach people on how they maximize digital in their day-to-day. This will not be a classroom training but rather a personal coach that follows e.g. the CEO around and advises during the day how to optimize digital solutions from AI to data to Snapchat.

Role 7: Business philosophers
Nature, the social impact, and the change in your company will put you into new dilemmas every day. Specially trained people will start supporting your business in new ethical decision making, business strategy, and what is right or wrong in a given context when data and facts cannot answer it.

(Tactic) Strength Theory

I am not entirely sure if the next item is linked to digital or generation or some other evolution, but it is a key item, nevertheless. You want a team where everyone is the best version of themselves.

Yet most individuals do not know their real strength. Our society is so much focused on improving the weakness. Of individuals that their strength is completely ignored. You do not want to major in minor things.
To explain how to staff your team we will use soccer as an analogy of people development coaching and organization.

Our goal is to prepare the best possible team that has the highest success rate of winning the champions league.

But first, you need to know your people.
While in a perfect world you know everything about your colleagues' all strengths and weaknesses and behavior motives, you only know their outside branding. We will come back to that later.

He who knows others is wise; he who knows himself is enlightened - Lao Tzu.

As many do know not even their own branding let us develop one for you together.

1. Draw a long straight line from top to bottom
2. Write down the two strengths you are strongest at? E.g. influencing or fast programming
3. Write down your two main weaknesses at the bottom of the line
4. Next, select 10 skills and place them on the line.

5. Presentation, digital technology knowledge (how it works and how to use), knowledge of the industry you are working in, project management, analytics advanced, excel, empathy, innovation & creativity, speed learning and memory, knowledge of the business and add a few more skills that are relevant to you.

6. Draw a horizontal line in the middle of the skills (if you have 10 then between the 5 and 6)

7. Evaluate if the order of your top/bottom three skills is correct

8. Take the top three and bottom three skills and phrase a branding sentence.

9. E.g. if your top skills are excel and analytics and your bottom skills are influencing and presentation then your branding statement would say: "the best analyst in excel and advanced analytics programming that the company has ever seen who is incapable of influencing people with their analytics by him/herself. Does that sound right to you? If yes, great! If not change your top skills. Do not change your weaknesses. Does it sound like a person you want to be or want to become? Most other people will only ever see your top and your bottom skills."

10. Look what you want to work on. Select 2 skills you want to work on in the next 4 months.

11. Most people select their weaknesses. Unfortunately, that is wrong. You can spend time on your weakness, but this will never evolve you and bring you to the next level. Imagine Lionel Messi or Ronaldo. Would you advise them to become better at goalkeeping? Even if they are great already at freekicks they will spend an unimaginable amount of time at training freekicks. You might say, that they should get better at defense but you really want to ensure they even grow further at scoring and playmaking. If you advise people to mostly work on their weaknesses, you will create the most average group as possible.

Remember that you are creating teams not just individuals. Weaknesses can easily be covered by the strength of others in the team.

Steve jobs do not have the reputation to be the best at treating people but in the end, his strengths were taking him over and beyond. It is more important that you have a team with diverse strengths than with a single harmonized profile. You want that the strength can cover the weaknesses of your team members and vice versa.

Today	Strength	Future
Disruptive Creation		
Connecting the dots		
Technology expertise		
Innovation (incl. Outside In)		
Strategic Thinking		
Analytics		
Change Management(indirect influencing)		
Interpersonal Skills		
Business (Core) knowledge		
Empathy		
Leadership		
Project Management		
Coding		
Stakeholder Management(directly influencing)		
Organizational Skills		
Visual Design (Visual Influencing)		
Overthinking		
Admin	Weakness	

(Tactic) Ikigai

Ikigai is a principle consisting of four questions that are supposed to help you answer the reason for which you wake up in the morning.
Ikigai comes from the Japanese: Iki = „Life ". Gai = „Worth"
In other words what makes life worth living. Ikigai is the crossing of four dimensions in which center the most optimal choice to fulfill your life is.

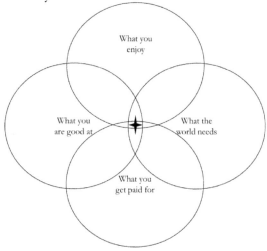

You are basically looking to find a part in your life that you enjoy, what the world needs, what you are good at, and what get paid for. If you cover only two of these aspects, you will be missing out. E.g. if you only select something that you are good at and you enjoy it might just be a hobby. If you select something you get paid for and the world needs, but you don't enjoy it is simply a profession but not fulfillment.

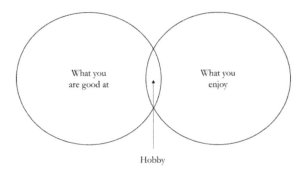

The easiest way is to exercise this with your team. Ask them to write down answers to the four questions and ask for each person to find what the central point between all of them is.

(Tactic) Innovative Disciplined Agility(IDA)

Part of your job is not to do your job. This oxymoronic statement is probably one of the most powerful ideas that unleash innovation. You always need to take the time to reflect and dream about how to change your world. If you are stuck in your day to day you will never take a step back and see how you can change it. It is your accountability to take the time of your job, stop doing your job so that finally you can do your job 10x faster. Innovative disciplined agility (IDA) is a principle that combines design thinking with an agile innovation cadence.

Opportunities multiply as they are seized – Sun Tzu

How Disciplined agility governance could save your investments?

Agile, another word that is being used by 100 people in 100 different ways. Hailed on the one hand as a solution to all project management issues and scorned as a never-ending development cycle without any results.
The best way how I have seen agile defined was twofold based on agile on a company level and agile on a project level

1) On company level: As the "Ability to capitalize on opportunities faster than everyone else".

"Agile for companies is the ability to capitalize on opportunities faster/ better than the competition."

---

2) On project level: as the adjustable but ultimately stable ratio between time, value and budget with dynamic individual values

---

"Agile for projects is the ability upscale/ descale a project scope or portfolio to generate the most optimal ratio between dynamic elements of the budget, time, and scope."

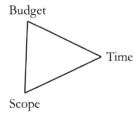

Budget

Time

Scope

Project management has gone through many changes and innovations. Today there are two main schools that are widely used in practice.
1) Waterfall - Linear Project management
2) Agile - Dynamic Project management

The waterfall is practically a linear process following the project phases of
Feasible- plan - design - build - test - product - support

The key phase of this type of project management in the design phase. You will have large workshops centers around collecting requirements, designing personas, documenting decisions, building flow charts, and PowerPoint slides showing how the result looks like. For existing solutions, you will do fit-gap analysis, thus overlaying which features of the solution are covering requirements and which gaps are existing that require you to adjust the solution.

Imagine your children would like Spaghetti Bolognese for dinner (their requirements), you see that in your kitchen you have the noodles, tomato but no beef. You either convince your customer (children) to change their needs. Good luck ...
or you go to the shop to buy meat (waterfall) or you use a vegan alternative that should cover the needs (something meaty, they probably do not taste the difference) and adapt to what you have a go in iterations = Agile.

Agile in its key idea allows adapting to change better, yet when it comes to projects for all its great aspects has one big downfall. Too often projects are changing scope often and are in an endless journey of sprints. Two key points that are often overlooked are the ability to manage the energy of the project and the ability to stop.

The word sprint comes obviously from the physical and sport relation of the word. High-energy focused effort on small pieces and short journeys instead of long development periods. The ability after each of the sprints to adjust is a great opportunity to not waste time and course correct. Yet imagine you were to go outside you go to the track stadium and you start sprinting. Not just once or twice but do 10-20 sprints after another. Moreover, imagine after each time you do a sprint you change direction. Sometimes a bit. Sometimes a lot. Project sprints will often feel like this for the project team. Agile is not the absence of planning. Agile for the most part requires even more planning than waterfall projects. Without a clear focus, a clear direction, and clear planning, agile is costing massive amounts of energy and what starts as a great concept often leads to failure due to the exhaustion of project members. The role of the coach and the project manager is always also to balance the projected trajectory combined with members' individual as well as group energy level to be successful in the long run.

A second differentiating factor to consider is the ability to stop. Projects in sprints often work like playing in a casino. Each time you play another hand of poker you run a sprint. You play a bit/ run a few sprints and when you feel you are on a good track you keep going. Sometimes this is the right thing but, in most cases, you need to know when to stop, when we should not run the next sprint and when to leave the table. In business-like, in the casino, we find it hard to leave the table when we are on a winning streak but even hard is once you are losing. You are down a few 100 Dollars at the table, but you keep hoping you are back. Just another hand. You think just need a bit more luck. Just one jackpot or just a royal flush. In the project, you often just look for one more sprint or one more project trial. But agile means to adopt and see when to stop and when to fold. You need to be able to read the playing field and the players at the table. In most businesses, we don't stop the project well. We continue until it becomes too costly to stop even if there is value remaining.

The second reason for the success of digital is discipline. Yet unfortunately, discipline is often misunderstood.
Discipline by many is considered something negative. Being disciplined is in many groups a synonym for corporal punishment. Or it is something that is put in connection with Germans and following rules.

A known method tried by many companies that are going for more agile is to create a companywide cadence. This means that e.g. each month or at least each quarter ALL ongoing projects are being reviewed and the projects that are not creating value get stopped especially if new projects get added that miss needed resources. Take a company like KBC they implemented such a cadence that was enabling them higher-level of agility in addition to more optimal resource allocation. Some companies take it to an extreme approach where they work with a fixed quota where each quarter 10% of projects need to stop. They create a forced ranking according to the value of the projects and cut the bottom projects. This had two key advantages. One, you stopped things. Two, many projects by themselves focused on delivering by end of each quarter as they knew the project might end anyway.

In the past, we have measured projects by being on time and on budget with the scope being adjusted whenever needed. Thus, the budget was fixed, time was fixed, and scope was variable in a normal waterfall project. In agile, the idea is that each dimension is variable. What is fix is the ratio between them.
You can create twice the value with twice the money, great!

You cannot create the expected value, reduce cost until you reach the original ratio of value, time, and cost.

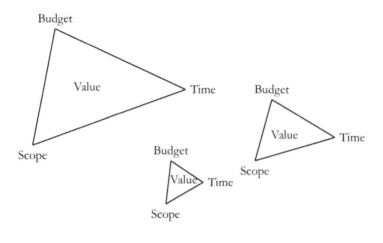

Create a quarterly cadence of all digital projects across all departments, create a forced ranking and cut the last 10%

Keep the ratio between time, budget and scope fix not the variables itself

---

Design thinking

Design thinking. You probably heard it, you might even have sent some of your team members to training or design thinking sessions. Design thinking is a nonlinear, iterative way that aims at understanding user needs, challenge ideas, create new solutions approaches, and build innovative products.

The first phase of design thinking is the emphasis phase, which aims at understanding the users' needs largely through observation, listening, and putting yourself in their shoes. You often observe users by sitting with them and follow them through the day, potentially filming how to act in a certain situation. A key differentiator to many other design processes or problem-solving approaches is the "feeling part" is as important as the objective analysis of the facts of the problem. Empathy is a key aspect of our daily life that we far too often missed in the business world.

We think too much and feel too little – Charlie Chaplin

The second phase is the "define phase". Here you start defining and redefining your problem. You might work with multiple personas to represent the perspective of each person. You will focus on framing and reframing the problem till you reach a problem statement. You will analyze all the information of the previous phase and try to connect the dots about the situation. Each problem should become a human-centered problem. It is not about the "company goal" but it is about the value for a certain type of person.

You will shift problems from "Why do only 5% of our digital sales come from customers that are elderly" to"Why do only 5% of elderly trust digital devices".

In the third phase, we will look at ideation. In this phase, very different techniques are being used ranging from brainstorming to other innovation idea frameworks.

In the fourth phase you prototype and in the 5th phase you test the solution with your target audience.

If you get stuck or have certain feedback you reiterate 2,3,4,5.

7 messages to rethink design thinking

Key message 1: Design thinking is not the solution to world hunger (of innovation)

Many different problems can get solved in many ways. The same is true for your employee's creativity. Not every process or framework will work for every employee. Design thinking has worked extremely well when it came to improving the experience of a user. Unfortunately, it also hinders challenging certain assumptions which often allows incremental but not disruptive changes. Due to the emphasis phase, you will think about how the users feel and how to improve the situation. But it creates three concreate issues

a) If your users that you analyze do not represent most users types you will be misled.

b) In business, the company itself might be your stakeholder, yet you cannot emphasize with a company as such. You might create solutions that work for the customer but are ultimately negative for your company's sustainability or contrary to your strategy.

c) You usually improve a process, but do not think how to completely remove/disrupt the process.

Key message 2: Do not get lost in „learning „ on the way

Failing in design thinking is an absolutely normal state of being and you will keep learning and improve each time. Yet don't get lost on the way. In any company's design thinking projects, all count as success as we learned, yet none have delivered any value. The spirit of design thinking is a great culture of learning, but it needs to be directed. Failing for the sake of failing creates disbelieve in the value of the project as well as fake change fatigue in your customers. Don't let design thinking become purely egocentric where the only persons who gain are project team members.

Key message 3: The Framework is a Framework

Design thinking is helping you to organize and helps you move along a path. It allows certain guidance and gives you the security to learn from others. Yet it is only a framework. Design thinking without the right employees, the right management commitment, and without an important problem to solve can never succeed. No matter how strong the framework might sound.

Key message 4: It needs to fit your culture

Culture eats strategy for breakfast. Culture eats frameworks for lunch. Culture eats change for dinner. Your company culture needs to allow the use of frameworks like design thinking. The more risk-minimizing a culture, the less the appetite for continuous improvement from management, and the fewer employees are rewarded for great ideas, the less likely your design thinking will succeed.

Key message 5: Forcing everyone to follow design thinking is just as limiting as forcing everyone in brainstorming sessions People are different - use it. Use design thinking where it makes sense with people who enjoy this way of working and do not enforce it as a general way of working. People, frameworks, and culture need to work together.

Key message 6: You need different backgrounds in your Team

Diversity of thought is the lifeblood of design thinking. If everyone is the same profile with the same background you will get the same idea. You might be surprised how ideas of students can disrupt century-long process chains with great ideas, how your HR people might be the best at advising your budget process improvements and your accountants might be the best at helping how to solve customer needs linked to their financial situation or otherwise.

Diversity does not just mean gender, but age, education, family situation, and professional background. If you can hire philosophy or psychology educated profiles into finance, commercial, or legal it will drive a massive boost in innovation and approach.

Key message 7: Evaluate if you are really making a difference

Learning requires you to see how things are truly are. Do not fall in the trap of celebrating success when there is none, don't hide failure. You should celebrate failure and learning but always measure if you really make an impact. Do not punish teams for not making an impact.
Yet failing and masking it as success is 10x worse than failing as it prevents learning and impacts the company culture.

(Tactic) Scalability

Digital is scalability. Cross geography. Cross country, Cross Department. Any solutions build should be built for scalability first. If you build e.g. a prediction tool, build it in a way that covers 80% of the countries for 80% of variables rather than building a solution that fits 1 country for 90%. Digital enables us to start small then scale to a large scale but only if we approach digital from a scalability point of view.

(Tactic) Innovate to negotiate

Not all innovations or innovative products are planned to stay. In many cases innovating is putting you into better negotiation positions. A sports shoe company might just enter the game of digital solutions or creating a separate personalization service (create your own shoe) next to an already existing web service. Even if only to put them into a better negotiation of terms of participating in the online service. Basically, you are saying in a normal case "you offer me a 10% royalty on the personalized shoes that are sold via your platform with a logo of our company. But we could also have our own personalization solution. We can merge our solution into yours or stop our service and redirect all our traffic to your page, but we need a 40% royalty instead." You innovate in a connected space only to negotiate a better position for your core products.

(Tactic) 7 top change management tactics
There are many different approaches to implementing change management as well as cultural transformation and it is a topic that can cover books. Yet here are some of the most effective "accelerator" techniques I have seen.

1) Day 0: Disruptive Co-Creation Staffing

Before you start your project, your change management starts by getting the right people into your project team. A right mix of vision, execution, and influence in the organization. The topic of co-creation is obviously a great way to get buy-in, but this is unfortunately only possible on a certain scale & in a certain context. In the project, I thought we did have a great idea to include a lot of internal customers and process owners to co-design a solution. After 3 days of workshops and design thinking sessions, we managed the design a solution that to 99% was mirroring the status -quo. Co-creating does not mean inclusion based on your role but also based on your mindset/capabilities to design the disruptions that are needed. You will never get the impact or excitement of a 1% change. And most likely it just means another company will disrupt you.

2) Day 1: Nostradamus Session

One of the most exciting techniques I use is the Nostradamus session. It helps greatly for reframing business questions, for change management and engagement building, and to going commitments.

The key principle is that you simulate the last day of your project. You will basically act out how the project will play out. Not just on an elevated level. Which means for analytical projects: Explain to a stakeholder the exact outcome that your analytics have found out.

Which means for assets: This is how someone needs to use the application at which point and why - but concretely explaining in detail which part of the application needs to be pressed, which decision needs to be taken.

Placing yourself in the future will help you to reframe if what you are asking is leading to success and how a stakeholder could react. You can then readjust on the one hand your message or even pivot your project & on the other hand to get stakeholder buy-in. If they commit to the project being in a certain end state it will be harder for them to resist later and make the transition a lot more fluent.

Here is how it works for Analytics Projects:

In this example, we are going to work on the project of "Identifying which employees will leave us and what we can do to prevent them". The target audience is the manager of the employees in question.

- You start by setting up your room. You will need to assign a presenter and a customer. If you can have a real model customer this will just improve the experience of the exercise. In our case, we assigned a person as the head of the IT department who has 150 people in his team.

- The project team as a group (excluding the customer) will work 15min on the example results of your project by making it specific to your customer.
  In this case, we are saying as example outcomes of the project which will give recommendations about the employees of the customer:
    - James will leave because we are not offering the new tesla as a company car
    - Julie will leave because she is in the same position for 3 years
    - Jake will leave because he is like his manager
    - Jamie will leave as she believes she is getting a too-low salary (despite she is within the midpoint)

- Jules will leave due to missing development opportunities
- ...

Try to find as many specific outcomes as possible in 15 min. Feel free to add controversial ones e.g. Julia will leave as she does not work for a woman.

- The presenter will share the above-mentioned points to the customer. The rest of the group will observe and evaluate the situation based on:
    - Can the customer act on most outcomes?
    - Is the customer willing to act on most outcomes?
    - Is the outcome connected to the strategy?
    - Is the value worth the effort it takes to implement the actions?

In the above case, it was seen that most actions could not be implemented by the "manager" of the employee. Thus, we needed to pivot towards a new customer within top management & HR.

Additionally, we saw that we might not want to take action as needed for the above cases for the complete company population. We needed to pivot the question towards «top talents». We are fine to increase the salary over proportionally for top talents but would not do this for the complete company including low performers.

Refine output until you reach a great outcome in the eyes of the complete team. Work backward from this outcome and reverse build your project plan and solution design

At the end of this exercise you will have a better-defined problem, a clear path forward, you already have a view how the future could look like and you actually have the first big step towards engagement and change management.

3) Day 2: Create Insta Influencer

Today more than TV advertisement products in the market get sold by influencers. YouTube, Instagram, Facebook, and many other platforms have helped Influencers to reach stardom.

The concept works so well because it is not the "producer" selling you something but someone you can connect to. We believe that someone that is closer to us has our best interests in mind.

For each of your projects, you should use the same also for internal projects, especially for internal projects. For your projects, you need to build your ambassadors or influencers to reach your customers from multiple directions or channels.

As a rule, the number of Influencers that you focus on should be the square root of the number of customers, as their impact is exponential.

$$Influencers = \sqrt{Customers}$$

- To reach 10 customers you should have 3.19 Influencers
- To reach 100 customers you need 10 influencers
- To reach 10000 customers you need 100 influencers

The downside of influencers is the reverse. If they do not like something they will try to block or prevent it at any step. Working with influencers means always hedging your bets. You want the right people included no matter the hierarchy or position, but they need to have a major influence in the organization and the mindset to be open for new ideas.

4) Day 10: Sex Moment Pitch

I once went to a conference that was horribly boring. I mean not just one speaker was boring but all. The venue was boring, the food was boring, and the program was boring. After the fifth speaker, I could see no one was listening. So, when the sixth speaker reaches the podium I did not listen even to his name or what I was about, I just wanted to leave. He started with a single slide and he caught everyone's attention. The slide said:

"What pharma can learn from PornHub"

The whole room was awake. Half because they did not expect this turn and half because they knew PornHub. The actual lesson had more to do with platform business and analytics and could have been covered by any platform like YouTube and did not cover any porn obviously, but it created a buzz. Everyone discussed the presentation after. I could still remember the content after.

Creating this buzz is such an amazing change management hack. Everyone wants to share and talk about it. It creates such an amazing basis for future communications and messages.

Now, in the business world, you will not often use such loaded comparisons, but you can use "lightning rod insights" or key items that shine. If you want to sell an AI show some of your customers a shining surprising insight and ask them not to share. One week later you will have half the management at your door asking about this AI and the insight that "no one" is supposed to know about.

5) Day 5: AB Testing in project

When I came from the university, I was excited about the idea of AB testing. The ability to implement an action or a campaign in one area of the company or a country but not in the other. After evaluating you will have a great unbiased fact-based view on if your actions have worked. Finally, you can measure the impact of marketing. Impact of projects and impact of messages in a coherent and factual manner.

Wrong.

Business reality has completely overruled my academic knowledge. In my first projects where we tried this, I realized at the end that the data did not convince anyone. Every time I received the message:

- "Only because it has worked in New York, does not mean it will work in Texas."
- "Only because it has worked in Finance it will work in Talent."

No matter how we structured the AB testing groups. There was always a cut/group that was used as an excuse.

The second reason why I realized it does not work in business is the large opportunity cost. Take two examples.

- The project is about identifying top talents and taking actions to prevent them from leaving
- The project is about new customer segmentation that was supposed to bring 100 million euro in sales

Each time when we discussed AB testing, we saw the following view:

- If we are right in our model, we will need to explain to our management that 50% of our top talents left, we knew it and we even knew how to prevent it - we just ignored it, to make a statistical point.
- We could have made a 100 million euro for our shareholders and have more customers enjoying the benefits of our product, but we decide to leave out the 50% because we wanted to make an impact assessment

AB testing after the project is working for

- Medical products where it is a requirement

- Projects where the benefits are not clear/small and the project team is not sure it will help solve the problem
- the AB testing point can long term generate 20x the value of the missed opportunity

If you are in option A or C, great. If you are in option b you might not even want to run the project.

The part that I have seen working is AB testing <u>within</u> the project. You create a very early prototype at the start of the project and directly implement the analytics or process or tool in a low-risk business area. The idea is not to use this test for your final communication and change management outside the team but within. It will help you refine and to prove to your own project team if what they have been building is actually a great product or insights. It will give you the confidence and belief to build a strong resilience that you will need to convince strong challengers of your project.

A surprising benefit is that you usually get support from the "low-risk areas in the business". For most projects, they are forgotten or considered less relevant to include in the projects yet bring a wealth of energy and knowledge to the table. A great example of under-utilized resources.

3) Day 20: Dressing Room Mirror

Whenever we go shopping with my girlfriend, she asks me in the dressing room if the mirror is making her slimmer. Shopping malls and shops have become very good at engaging their customers to buy cloth, largely by making them feel better. By giving them the feeling of looking great. Even if it meant to slightly adjust the perception. Change management is largely about making people transition in a positive way and sometimes we need to help them do it.

In the business context, this also applies to your own stakeholders, especially those higher in the organization.

In one project which handled the implementation of an AI system to drastically improve the recruitment services of the company. Initially, the change was met with resistance. "Why do we need to change? Today we are already within the benchmark of our recruitment times. It's not our fault its sometimes going slow." This was the reaction after approaching the pitch from a technology angle. It was perceived as an efficiency and quality improvement tool but not as something that will help them.

So, we had to change the message. We reframed the project as: "What if, YOU can become the world's best recruitment team. What if YOU can reduce the recruitment time for top candidates from applying online to the point, they have the interview with the hiring manager from the original 3 weeks average to 3 hours by using this AI. You have control of the AI at each step, and we can help you make this into reality." By further explaining how the tool helps them archive a higher status it was turned into an amazing collaboration.

6) Day 30: Burn the boats

Corona has done one of the best change management activities I have ever seen. Change management to go digital. Change management that suddenly the home office can be effective. Change management that we do not need cars every day. And it did it largely without communication but by burning the boats.

By removing the alternative.

Seen as a nuclear option in change management it is hard but effective. In the past, companies used to run many proofs of concepts, but they always allowed to not make the transition and framed the change as optional.

People look for real change. Everyone supports POC because they do not do harm, but they also do not help change.

If you want people to switch from one system to the other system or new way of working, shut down the old system. It should only be done in special cases, but some changes require the right level of force. You just cannot overdo it, as it will spoil your relationship with your team. This also works towards your customers.

You might remember when Apple got rid of the plug for earphones or got rid of the fingerprint unlock mode. We all transitioned towards the air pods and facial unlocking impressing quickly. If Apple would have allowed a parallel run, this might have taken a very long time for people to adjust.

(Tactic) The next cycle

Success happens in the next cycle. The earlier you catch a trend the better position it puts you in.

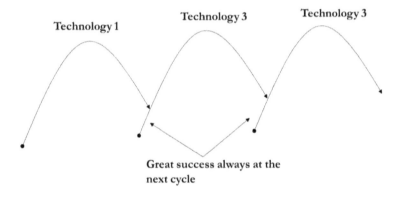

Technology 1
Technology 3
Technology 3

Great success always at the next cycle

Many companies have trend-watchers, as well as innovation lab teams, focused on finding the next big thing. There are a few focus points that can help identify trends.

Firstly, failure is predicting success. Trends are seen first by failures. A great way to see trends is about where the most failures are. Look for failed patents, look for areas of most failed startups. Here you will find the next big success.

Secondly, watch for trend breaks. Corona has massively changed our ways of being that other trends will do the same. Watch closely how the behaviors in the next weeks will changes e.g. by watching website trends or google search word changes.

Thirdly, look at how the consumer will evolve in the next 10 years.

Here is some of my research about customers in countries like UK, US, Germany

The consumer in 2030
- Takes 35% of all education are online, most first years at universities will study from home
- Is more interest in a circular economy than any generation before
- Is open to sharing data when it serves a purpose
- 80% have two or more social media accounts
- 12% of products are 3D printed or have 3D printed parts
- 20% interact with VR or AR monthly (especially gaming & education)
- 75% interact with AI systems every week
- 25% have AI colleagues / complete AI processes at work
- Is using 50 digital devises (mobile, wearables, IoT)
- Loves extreme individualization
- Everything as a service extreme with a new rise in microservices
- We will have thousands of approved healthcare algorithms for diagnosis, prevention of diseases and treatment optimization
- 350k organs will be 3D printed
- Cost of sensors will be 1% of today's cost enabling even more intelligent devices

- 35% of the workforce will be digital natives which especially in digital late bloom areas like politics, healthcare, and banking will accelerate the change coming towards these sectors and creating an openness towards transformation
- Data ethics and protection will go through multiple circles and will balance off. Between data sharing as an industry enabler and data privacy as prevention from state control

Finally, allow me to do a few predictions about what will happen in digital in the next 8-10 years. Knowing that this is a perspective and will be wrong, it might help to frame your own opinions about the future.

- China will launch a blockchain variant digital currency called CBDC in 2021. The financial access in the country will reach 75% by 2025 and will create unimaginable policy options in global trade, breaking the US pressure, combined with the fact that China as an innovation hub will not bring their companies to the US Wallstreet, making china one more time attractive as a global player

- AI & cloud will change gaming drastically. Due to app streaming, there will be no need for the next PlayStation or Xbox. Rather game hardware will be sold surround laptops or tablets. You will stream games not own them anymore

- AI will change games in a way that games will adjust to the player's preferences and learns which part of a game the player likes to create unique experiences. No two players will have the same experience

- Amazon will be the most important health player including that they will become the world's first "virus-free delivery chain" and they will lead healthcare testing capacity for the next corona as well as say day medical supply

- SAP Hana and Netezza will go out of the market as they are replaced by contextualized databases

- Disney will win battles in streaming in the first 5 years especially due to their content access but will be overcome by Amazon in terms of content and infrastructure with 75% of American households will have amazon prime afterward

- Zoom and Slack and Spotify will be bought if they become too big by IBM, Microsoft, and Facebook

- If they stay small Microsoft will invest in them to ensure the perception of a non-monopoly market

- The next big drug will come from biohacking from a below 30-year-old with biohacking skills

- Main tech players will stop general-purpose facial recognition sales. While Amazon and Microsoft will stop sales of AI to police for 2 years it will restart sales in 2023 due to missing alternatives and too many smaller players covering the area anyway with the argument "better controlled ethical AI managed by the big players than low-cost facial recognitions software from small players".

- You will get 100% personalized prices

- AI & drones will be at the core of the kill chain at National Defence, on how to read and control populations

- Google will find cures for 10 diseases before pharma companies will

- Walmart or Amazon will open a real-world micro service market within their mobile /service infrastructure covering services like cleaning apartments, groceries, shopping advice, gardening, construction, hairstylist, and many more, while apple will open such a market for art, music, photography and creative services

- The war of talent will become more globalized due to the new "working from anywhere" trend

- In 2030 delivery will reach a new level as the first products bought online will be instantly 3D printed at the home of the customer. You want a new shoe. Order and print within 2 hours

- Robotics will be taxed but not enough. As the market that taxes the most will lose most of the industries

The final hand

You are back at the digital poker table. Only this time you are better prepared. This time you know your cards, you know the rules, and you know how to play the odds.

In your hand, you hold a platform card and an artificial intelligence card. You understand that they are some of the top cards of the future in your hand. You bet big because you understand that in a game where the risk is high we can control the payout and the likelihood to win. You know that your bets will overcome failures if you play enough games and adopt. Each game you are learning. Each game you understand more.

You start being able to read the opponents. You start understanding that your neighbor who is talking about his RPA card as an AI has no clue what he is talking about. Easy money.

Other players have bigger pockets, but you have the right strategy and right tactics for each of them. In each game, you are playing the people as much as you play the cards.

Throughout the night, you win and lose. You know that failure is part of it but it does not worry you. You stay calm, you have a strategy. You calmly play your cards the best you can. You play towards your strength. As a digital leader, you trust what your team has told you to prepare and you are resilient.

In one game everyone is folding their cards as the big player on the table is showing off. But you can see behind this. You know he is bluffing. You play your tactic based on the right anchor and you know he is biased towards his past success. You take the pot. Digital scalability and quick adaptability are more important than size. Size matters but only if they would be able to focus it.

In another game, you realize your opponent only plays one card. Your opponent is the best at digitalization. Whereas you have a whole portfolio of cards. You have a balance. Your balanced portfolio will outperform his.

Over time your competition notices that you are always a step ahead of them. Your augmented decision making and AI systems help you make smart decisions at each hand. So, others start duplicating what you are doing. But you stay calm, you have a strategy. Only too late they realize that even when they use AI, you surround it with game theory and a strong strategy, where they try to win on "best practice alone".

Some people start leaving the table. They lost their digital bets.

Late in the game, a new player enters. One of the tech giants. Everyone is scared and surprised. But you stay calm, you have a strategy. While others are taken out by the tech giant you are playing on well as you partnered with the tech giant at the right time and proved your value in this environment.

You play all night till you reach the final hand.
On the table, you have a digital transformation card, an AI card, and a quantum computing card. The room is tense. Everyone is staring at you. Everyone looks at you. But you stay calm, you have a strategy.

Then the unexpected happens. Your opponent plays a royal flush. The top highest value cards together. The audience in the room is stunned. Everyone knows who the winner is.

You show your cards. It takes a moment to sink in but at this moment you played cards no one has ever seen. You brought a new digital business model on the table that no one has ever seen. At this moment even your opponent understands: You just changed the game.

You changed the odds; you won the digital jackpot.

Are you ready to make this a reality in your business?

Glossary

API = Application programming interface
MDM = Master Data Management
CRM = Customer Relationship Management
AWS = Amazon webservices
QC = Quantum Computing
DL = Deep Learning
SAP = Company mostly known for the ERP system
ERP = Enterprise Resource Planning
OCR = Optical character recognition
KM = Knowledge management
AI = Artificial Intelligence
AR = Augmented Reality
VR = Virtual Reality
OPEX = Operational Expenses

Dedicated to those that taught me

www.ingramcontent.com/pod-product-compliance
Lightning Source LLC
LaVergne TN
LVHW041203050326
832903LV00020B/438